Collins
Road
Atlas
Spain &
Portugal

Contents

2 – 10	Driving in Spain
11 – 18	Driving in Portugal
19	Regional map of Spain & Portugal
20	Distance chart
21	Key to map pages
22 – 59	Road maps 1:1 000 000
60 – 62	City through–route maps
60	Barcelona
61	Lisboa, Madrid
62	Sevilla, Valencia
63 – 88	Index to place names

Driving in Spain

The most noticeable aspect of Spanish driving is the overuse of the car horn. Although in general driving standards are quite good, drivers do tend to be impatient, particularly in traffic jams. The minimum age for driving in Spain is 18. There are strict laws on drink-driving. If bringing your car into Spain, you will need your vehicle registration document and driving licence. You may also need a Green Card, available from your insurer in the UK for a small fee. Within the EU your general UK car insurance covers you. You may want to take out extra breakdown cover (AA or RAC).

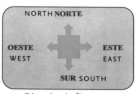

▲ **Direction indicators**

▼ **Speed restrictions**

built up area	50 km/h
ordinary roads	90 km/h
dual carriageway	120 km/h
motorway	120 km/h

▲ **City centre**

▲ Spanish numberplate. **E** is for **España**

Green and E- is a European route and a main road — **E-4**

Red with N- is a dual carriageway (**autovía**; these function also as motorways) — **N-401**

Blue with A- is a motorway, **autopista** — **A-28**

Orange with C- is a primary road — **C-607**

Green with C- is a secondary road — **C-170**

Yellow with C- is a third- class road — **C-241**

Orange with a D- indicates a deviation; follow this to rejoin your original route — **D-7**

▲ **Colour-coding for Spanish road signs**

◄ **Speed limit controlled by radar**
There are on-the-spot fines for traffic offences, notably speeding and drink-driving – and credit cards are accepted!

white: major route signposted from a town

yellow: places of interest to visitors; the port

green: street names

major route signposted from a town; to the **Autovía**

a place of interest to visitors; parking

▲ In cities and towns, the colour coding on road signs changes

▲ Few drivers stop at zebra crossings. An oncoming driver flashing their lights does NOT mean 'after you'; it will probably mean 'I'm coming through'.

▲ Pedestrian zone   ▲ End of pedestrian zone

 ◄ Forbidden to all vehicles – pedestrian zone

 ◄ Vía Preferente indicates a bus and taxi lane

 ◄ Lorry exit

we are going to…
vamos a…
ba-mos a…

is the road good?
¿está bien la carretera?
es-ta byen la kar-re-te-ra

is the pass open?
¿está abierto el puerto?
es-ta a-byer-to el pwer-to

which is the best route?
¿cuál es la mejor ruta?
kwal es la me-khor roo-ta

can you show me on the map
¿puede indicarmelo en el mapa?
pwe-de een-dee-kar-me-lo en el ma-pa

do we need snow chains?
¿hace falta usar cadenas?
a-the fal-ta oo-sar ka-de-nas

Talking

Some motorways (**autopistas**) are free and some carry toll charges (which can be expensive). Look out for the sign **peaje** (toll). Payment is due on completion of each sector covered. You do not receive tickets. These toll motorways are similar to UK motorways but aren't usually as busy. Non-toll motorways, however, are more like dual carriageways with numerous exits. They offer a great number of possibilities for stopping, ranging from simple café/bars to restaurants, hotels and petrol stations. There are also big service stations with full facilities (cash dispensers, mini-markets, play areas, etc.), but they are few and far between.

▲ Spanish motorways are signposted in blue. The speed limit is 120kph. Motorway info website is **www.aseta.es**

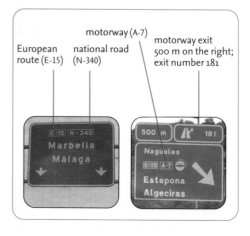

motorway (A-7)

European route (E-15)   national road (N-340)   motorway exit 500 m on the right; exit number 181

◀ Toll

Before you reach the toll booth there will be a sign showing which cards are accepted for payment. ▼

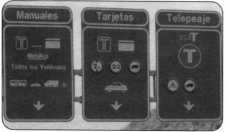

▲ At the toll stop you have a choice of payment: either cash (**Manuales**) for all vehicles (**metálico** means cash), card (**Tarjetas**) or prepaid (**Telepeaje**).

◄ Services are available on taking the 162 exit. Service stations are known as **Areas de Servicio**.

▲ The amount will be displayed at the booth. The front passenger will be closest in a right-hand drive car.

◄▲ Roadside SOS phones have instructions in English, French and German as well as Spanish.

▲ **Card-only lane for payment**

If you break down on the motorway

There is a very small or no hard shoulder on Spanish motorways. If you have to stop or you break down, you must pull over as far as you can, put on your hazard lights and place your warning triangle 50 metres behind the vehicle. (It should be visible for at least 100 metres). Both **autopistas** and **autovías** have SOS emergency phones located at about 1500-metre intervals. You simply press the button and wait for assistance.

my car has broken down
se me ha averiado el coche
se me a a-ber-ya-do el ko-che

what should I do?
¿qué hago?
ke a-go

I am on my own
estoy sola
es-toy so-la

my children are in the car
los niños están en el coche
los neen-yos es-tan en el ko-che

the car is...
el coche está...
el ko-che es-ta...

before junction...
antes de la salida...
an-tes de la sa-lee-da...

after junction...
después de la salida...
des-pwes de la sa-lee-da...

registration number...
matrícula...
mat-ree-koo-la...

it is a blue fiat
es un fiat azul
es oon fee-yat a-thool

Spanish drivers will often park their car wherever their fancy takes them. Be warned that whilst this is common, it is still illegal. In general, parking can be a problem almost everywhere. The safest option is to find a multi-storey or pay-and-display area. There are restrictions regarding parking and these are clearly indicated. Cars may be towed away if parked in a restricted area. This is more common than clamping. If your car has been towed away you will have to pick it up from the local council compound, give details of the car and pay the fine. Police or traffic wardens will know where the local compound is. Semi-official parking attendants will often assist you in finding parking spaces on the street. A small tip of around 1 euro is expected.

▲ Signs for pay-and-display machines ▲

▲ Residents' parking only

▼ Pay and display machine

— coins (**monedas**)

tariffs (**tarifas**)

times when parking restrictions apply (**horarios**)

no change is given (**no devuelve cambio**)

to cancel (**cancelar**)

press for ticket

▲ No parking at all except disabled

▼ 24-hour parking

per night

TARIFAS APARCAMIENTO	
Charges ►	
first half hour or part of	PRIMERA HORA Ó FRACCION 1,00 €
each further half hour or part of	CADA HORA RESTANTE Ó FRACCION 0,75 €
maximum 24 hours	MÁXIMO 24 HORAS 15,00 €
(including VAT) in force from 1 January 2002	IVA INCLUIDO EN VIGOR A PARTIR DEL DÍA 1 DE ENERO DEL 2.002

▲ Be careful: **libre** means 'spaces' not 'free of charge'. **Completo** means full. ▼

parking only for cars and motorbikes

caravans and lorries forbidden

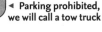

◄ Parking prohibited, we will call a tow truck

▲ Pay point

No parking ► on Thursdays from 8 am–3 pm for a street market

◄ No parking weekdays 9 am– 2 pm and 4 pm–8 pm except for loading and unloading

---

where is the best place to park?
¿cuál es el mejor sitio para aparcar?
*kwal es el me-**khor** **seet**-yo **pa**-ra a-par-**kar***

where is there a car park?
¿dónde hay un aparcamiento?
***don**-de aee oon a-par-ka-**myen**-to*

can I park here?
¿se puede aparcar aquí?
*se **pwe**-de a-par-**kar** a-**kee***

the ticket machine doesn't work
no funciona el parquímetro
*no foonth-**yo**-na el par-**kee**-met-ro*

how long for?
¿cuánto tiempo?
***kwan**-to **tyem**-po*

Petrol stations are essentially the same as those in the UK. Although self-service (**autoservicio**) is common, many petrol stations still have pump attendants. Most accept credit cards. Be aware that leaded petrol still exists in Spain and you must ask for unleaded petrol (**sin plomo**) which is always coloured green. Many petrol stations offer a lot of services other than just providing petrol (car wash, air, water, etc.). Car washes are very similar in style and format all over Spain. Valet cleaning is generally not available. You will probably have to pay for air and sometimes water.

▲ Colour-coded pumps: black for diesel (**gasóleo**), green for unleaded (**sin plomo**) and red for leaded (**super**)

▼ Vacuum

— hand wash &
— oil change
— 4th floor

◄ Air

no money!
This machine is emptied daily

automatically balanced and inflated pressure (choose button for precise bar pressure measurement)

bar counter (to measure pressure manually)

manually balanced and inflated pressure (adjust using buttons)

where is there a petrol station?
¿dónde hay una gasolinera?
don-de aee oo-na ga-so-lee-ne-ra

...worth of unleaded petrol
...de gasolina sin plomo
...de ga-so-lee-na seen plo-mo

the card for the carwash
la tarjeta para el autolavado
la tar-khe-ta pa-ra el ow-to-la-ba-do

fill it up please
lleno por favor
lyen-o por fa-bor

pump number...
surtidor número...
soor-tee-dor noo-me-ro...

how much is that?
¿cuánto es?
kwan-to es

If you are a member of a motoring organisation, such as the AA or RAC, you will have access to Real Automobil Club de España, Spain's national motoring organisation. This round-the-clock national emergency call-out service is based in Madrid. You can contact them on 91 593 33 33. You may need to contact your cover organisation in the UK to check if you have to pay a supplement for this or not. Kwik-Fit type fitters are few and far between in Spain but look out for 'Feu–Vert' signs (French-owned equivalent).

TALLER MECANICO
GRUA PERMANENTE 24 HORAS
SERVICIO NEUMÁTICOS TURISMO
TLFNS: 926 33 91 15 - 926 33 93 40

◄ **Garage for repairs**
This one offers 24-hour pick-up truck and tyre service for cars.

I have broken down
tengo una avería
ten-go oo-na a-be-ree-ya

the car won't start
el coche no arranca
el ko-che no ar-ran-ka

the battery is flat
la batería está descargada
la ba-te-ree-ya es-ta des-kar-ga-da

I have a flat tyre
tengo una rueda pinchada
ten-go oo-na rwe-da peen-cha-da

I need new tyres
necesito neumáticos nuevos
neth-es-ee-to ne-oo-ma-tee-kos nwe-bos

I have run out of petrol
me he quedado sin gasolina
me e ke-da-do seen ga-so-lee-na

where is there a garage?
¿dónde hay un garaje?
don-de aee oon ga-ra-khe

something is wrong with...
algo le pasa a(l)...
al-go le pa-sa a(l)...

the ... is not working
el/la ... no funciona
el/la ... no foonth-yo-na

the ... are not working
los/las ... no funcionan
los/las ... no foonth-yo-nan

can you repair it?
¿puede arreglarlo?
pwe-de ar-re-glar-lo

how long will it take?
¿cuánto tardan en arreglarlo?
kwan-to tar-dan en ar-re-glar-lo

when will it be ready?
¿para cuándo estará?
pa-ra kwan-do es-ta-ra

how much will it cost?
¿cuánto me costará?
kwan-to me kos-ta-ra

can you replace the windscreen?
¿me puede cambiar el parabrisas?
me pwe-de kamb-yar el pa-ra-bree-sas

please change...
¿me cambia...?
me kamb-ya...

the oil
el aceite
el a-they-te

the tyres
los neumáticos
los ne-oo-ma-tee-kos

Talking

Emergency (Spain)

The Spanish police is in 3 parts: **Guardia Civil** (for countryside, roads and borders), **Policía Nacional** (for provincial capitals and large towns) and **Policía Municipal/local** (for local bylaws). The **Guardia Civil** deal with traffic accidents and offences, but local parking offences fall to the **Policía Municipal**. All carry guns. Generally speaking, you may find the local police the easiest and most relaxed to deal with. The emergency number for the local police is 092. If you have to report an accident, etc., you will have to fill in a form at the local police station. This will be in Spanish.

help!
¡socorro!
so-kor-ro

can you help me!
¿me puede ayudar?
me pwe-de a-yoo-dar

please call...
por favor llame a...
por fa-bor lya-me a...

the police
la policía
la po-lee-thee-ya

an ambulance
una ambulancia
oo-na am-boo-lanth-ya

fire!
¡fuego!
fwe-go

please call the fire brigade!
por favor llame a los bomberos
por fa-bor lya-me a los bom-be-ros

my ... has been stolen
me han robado...
me an ro-ba-do...

I want to report a theft
quiero denunciar un robo
kyer-o de-noon-thyar oon ro-bo

here are my insurance details
aquí tienen mis datos del seguro
a-kee tyen-en mees da-tos del se-goo-ro

where is the police station/the hospital?
¿dónde está la comisaría/el hospital?
don-de es-ta la kom-ee-sa-ree-ya/el os-pee-tal

I would like to phone...
quería llamar a...
kee-ree-ya lya-mar a...

my car has been broken into
me han entrado en el coche
me an en-tra-do en el ko-che

please give me your insurance details
¿me puede dar sus datos del seguro?
me pwe-de dar soos da-tos del se-goo-ro

I need a report for my insurance
necesito un informe para el seguro
neth-e-see-to oon een-for-me pa-ra el se-goo-ro

Driving in Portugal

If you are taking your own car into Portugal you will need your driving licence, registration documents, insurance, breakdown cover and ID (passport). Driving in Portugal can be a harrowing experience, with overtaking on bends, tailgating and drink-driving all common. As in many southern European countries, impatience is rife, with over-use of the horn, although road-rage is quite rare.

▲ Blue **auto-estrada** sign with km markers

▲ Red **main highway** sign

▲ Ordinary **main-road** sign

▲ **Original main road**

▲ **Urban highway**

▲ **Pictogram** on road signs indicating the town centre

▼ **Speed restrictions**

built up area	50 km/h
main roads	100 km/h
motorway	120 km/h

▲ **Portuguese number plate**
P on the blue panel is for Portugal, and the last 2 letters indicate the district of registration.

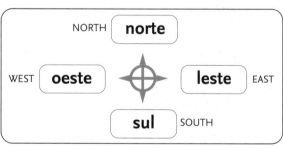

▲ **Direction indicators**

we are going to...
vamos a...
vah-moosh uh...

how many kilometres is it?
quantos quilómetros são?
kwan-toosh kee-loh-muh-troosh sowñ

how do I get to the motorway?
como se vai para a auto-estrada?
koh-moo suh vy pa-ruh uh ow-too-shtrah-duh

which is the best route?
qual é o melhor caminho?
kwa-le oo mel-yor ka-meen-yoo

can you show me on the map?
pode-me indicar no mapa?
pod-muh een-dee-kar noo mah-puh

Talking

▲ Signs you will see on entering (above) and leaving (below) villages. ▼

▲ **Tolls** are payable on motorways and Lisbon bridges.

▲ 30 km/h limit

▲ End of 30 km/h limit

◄ No parking 9am to 7pm except loading and unloading

Signs show which vehicles can use certain lanes on particular days. ▼

▲ Services area (Grândola)

Toll machine
Press the red button ▼ and take your ticket.

SAÍDA
▲ exit

TODAS AS DIRECÇÕES
▲ all routes

DEVAGAR
▲ slow down

Talking

is this the road to... ?
esta é a estrada para...?
esht e uh shtrah-duh pa-ruh...

I am sorry, I did not know that...
desculpe, não sabia que...
dush-koolp nowñ suh-bee-uh kuh...

I could not park here
não é permitido estacionar aqui
nowñ e pur-mee-tee-doo shtas-yoo-nar a-kee

how do I get to... ?
como se vai para...?
koh-moo suh vy pa-ruh...

it is a one-way street
é sentido único
e sayñ-tee-doo oo-nee-koo

there is a ... speed limit
tem um limite de...
tayñ ooñ lee-mee-tay duh...

There are a number of motorways (**auto-estradas**) in Portugal. They are toll roads, as are the two bridges into Lisbon from the south. You pay at the toll booth. **Via Verde** is for drivers who subscribe to the automatic express electronic toll service. SOS phones are available for emergency breakdown assistance on motorways.

▲ Blue motorway (**auto-estrada**) signs indicate road numbers and destinations. E indicates this is also a European route.

◄ **auto-estrada**
Motorway sign

2 markers = **safety**

1 marker = **danger**

▲ Chevron-shaped distance warnings are painted on some motorways. Drivers are meant to keep 2 markers behind the car in front.

◄ Overhead **Via Verde** indicator. Do not drive in these lanes.

If you break down on the motorway

If you break down on the motorway, you should put on your hazard warning lights and place your warning triangle about 100m behind the car. Then make your way to the emergency phone. An arrow on the distance indicator will show you which way the nearest phone is. It is never more than 1km away. The police will arrange for a recovery vehicle to come to you.

my car's broken down
tenho o carro avariado
ten-yoo oo kar-roo a-vuhr-yah-doo

what should I do?
que devo fazer?
kuh dev-oo fa-zehr

I am on my own
estou só
shtoh soh

it is a blue Fiat
é um Fiat azul
e ooñ fee-at a-zool

the registration number is…
a matricula é…
uh mah-tree-koo-luh e…

the car is…
o carro está…
oo kar-roo shta…

after exit…
depois da saída…
duh-poysh duh sah-ee-duh…

before exit…
antes da saída…
an-tesh duh sah-ee-duh…

Parking can be a real problem in Portuguese towns. You may commonly come across cars parked in strange places, as Portuguese drivers often pull in regardless of conditions. It is safer to look for signs to parking areas and pay a small fee, than end up with a **multa** (fine) or be towed away. Disabled parking spaces are scarce. In busy areas you may see young men and boys finding spaces for drivers. They may look scruffy, but they are also quick to spot gaps and guide you in. Just remember, they expect a tip.

RETIRE AQUI O SEU BILHETE — get your ticket here

▲ Pay and Display sign

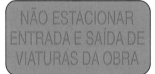

▲ no parking
entrance and exit of works vehicles

Premir para abrir
Press to open

Here, the driver presses the red button for a ticket to open the barrier to the car park.

pay here ▶
On-street parking meter sign

payment zone ▶

dias úteis = weekdays

sábados = Saturdays

zona **P** pago

dias úteis: 08 às 20h
sábados: 08 às 13h

In larger towns, ▶
parking may be underground.

spaces
Livre means spaces, not that parking is free!

full

private

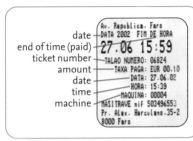

date
end of time (paid)
ticket number
amount
date
time
machine

▲ Place your parking ticket on display in your car

PARQUE DE ESTACIONAMENTO
PREÇÁRIO
8.00-20.00 horas

▲ car park prices 8am to 8pm

TARIFAS

▲ tariffs

◄ towaway zone

▼ Many automatic machines in Portugal have an English language option

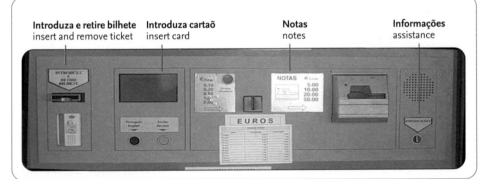

Introduza e retire bilhete
insert and remove ticket

Introduza cartaõ
insert card

Notas
notes

Informações
assistance

where's the best place to park?
onde é o melhor sitio para estacionar?
*oñ-duh e oo mel-**yor** **seet**-yoo **pa**-ruh shtass-yoo-**nar***

can I park here?
posso estacionar aqui?
pos**-soo shtass-yoo-**nar** a-**kee

do I need to pay?
tenho que pagar?
ten**-yoo kuh puh-**gar

how long for?
por quanto tempo?
*poor **kwan**-too **teñ**-poo*

the ticket machine doesn't work
o paquímetro não funciona
*oo pa-**kee**-may-troo nowñ foonss-**yoh**-nuh*

Talking

Most filling stations operate in the same way as in the UK, with self-service pumps, although in smaller areas you will still find one- or two-pump garages which are attended. Filling stations are scarce in rural areas. Note, when you are filling up your car, that diesel is **gasóleo** and petrol is **gasolina**.

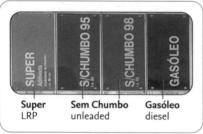

Super	**Sem Chumbo**	**Gasóleo**
LRP	unleaded	diesel

▲ **Pumps are colour coded**

You can pay with major credit cards (listed on the side of the machine) and instructions are in Portuguese and English...▼

Larger stations ▶ have pre-pay machines. You key in before you begin how much you want to pay.

Pre-fixed amount
1 Don't remove nozzle
2 Press buttons as required
3 Confirm on the keypad the amount required
4 Remove nozzle, fill up, and pay at the cash desk

air ▶ and water

switch off ▶ engine

Talking

where is the nearest petrol station?
onde é a estação de serviço mais perto?
*oñ-duh e uh shta-**sowñ** duh sehr-**vee**-soo mysh **pehr**-too*

... euros worth of unleaded petrol
... euros de gasolina sem chumbo
*... **eur**-oosh duh ga-zoo-**lee**-nuh sayñ **shoom**-boo*

number...
número...
noo-muh-roo...

fill it up, please
encha, por favor
*eñ-shuh poor fa-**vor***

please check the oil
pode verificar o óleo, por favor
*pod vuh-ree-fee-**kar** oo ol-yoo poor fa-**vor***

If you belong to a driving organisation and have European cover, you will be able to use ACP, the Portuguese breakdown service. Otherwise, you will have to rely on local garages.

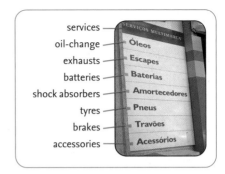

- services — Óleos
- oil-change — Óleos
- exhausts — Escapes
- batteries — Baterias
- shock absorbers — Amortecedores
- tyres — Pneus
- brakes — Travões
- accessories — Acessórios

my car has broken down
o meu carro está avariado
oo may-oo kar-roo shta a-va-ree-ah-doo

the battery is flat
a bateria está descarregada
uh ba-tuh-ree-uh shta dush-kar-ruh-ga-duh

I have a flat tyre
tenho um furo
ten-yoo ooñ foo-roo

where is the nearest garage?
onde é a oficina mais perto?
oñ-duh e uh o-fee-see-nuh mysh pehr-too

the ... is not working
o/a ... não funciona
oo/uh ... nowñ foons-yoh-nuh

can you repair it?
pode arranjá-lo?
pod ar-rañ-zha-loo

when will it be ready?
quando estará pronto?
kwañ-doo shta-ra proñ-too

can you replace the windscreen?
pode substituir o pára-brisas?
pod sub-shteet-weer oo pa-ruh-bree-zush

do you have the parts?
tem as peças?
tayñ ush pes-ush

it won't start
não pega
nowñ peg-uh

it won't go
não anda
nowñ añ-duh

I've run out of petrol
não tenho gasolina
nowñ ten-yoo gaz-oo-lee-nuh

the ... are not working
os/as ... não funcionam
oosh/ush ... nowñ foons-yoh-nowñ

how long will it take?
quanto tempo leva?
kwañ-too teñ-poo leh-vuh

how much will it cost?
quanto vai custar?
kwañ-too vy koosh-tar

is it serious?
é grave?
e grav

Emergency (Portugal)

The emergency number 112 connects you to any of the emergency services (**Polícia, Bombeiros, Ambulância**). It is operated in Portuguese, French and English. There are several branches of the police: **GNR** (National Guard, military); **PSP** (Public Security Police), **Brigada de Trânsito** (Traffic Police), the **PJ** (Crimefighters) and **Guarda Fiscal** (Customs & Excise).

◄ GNR station

Bombeiros
fire brigade
▼

▼ PSP station

help!
socorro!
*soo-**kor**-roo*

can you help me!
pode-me ajudar?
pod**-muh a-joo-**dar

call...
chame...
shahm...

the police
a polícia
*uh poo-**lees**-yuh*

an ambulance
uma ambulância
*oo-muh am-boo-**lans**-yuh*

there's a fire!
há fogo!
*a **foh**-goo*

call the fire brigade!
chame os bombeiros!
*sham oosh bom-**bay**-roosh*

someone has stolen my...
roubaram-me...
*roh-**ba**-rowñ-muh...*

my money
o dinheiro
*oo deen-**yay**-roo*

my passport
o passaporte
*oo pas-sa-**port***

here are my insurance details
aqui está o meu seguro
*a-**kee** shta oo **may**-oo suh-**goo**-roo*

how much is the fine?
quanto é a multa?
***kwañ**-too e uh **mool**-tuh*

I'm lost
estou perdido(a)
*shtoh puhr-**dee**-doo(-duh)*

I've been raped
fui violado(a)
*fwee vee-oh-**lah**-doo(-duh)*

where is the police station?
onde é a esquadra?
***oñ**-duh e uh **shkwa**-druh*

I want to report a theft
quero participar um roubo
***keh**-roo par-tee-see-**par** ooñ **roh**-boo*

my car has been broken into
assaltaram-me o carro
*sa-sal-**ta**-rown-muh oo **kar**-roo*

I need a report for my insurance
preciso dum relatório para o meu seguro
*pruh-**see**-zoo dooñ ruh-la-**tor**-yoo pa-ruh oo **may**-oo suh-**goo**-roo*

Regional map of Spain & Portugal

Capital city: **Madrid**

▲ Spain

Capital city: **Lisboa**

▲ Portugal

▼ **Internet links**

Tourist information

www.tourspain.es
www.portugalinsite.pt
www.portugal-info.net
www.met-office.gov.uk
www.bbc.co.uk/weather

Motoring information

www.asecap.com
www.brisa.pt
www.mir.es/telonext/index.htm
http://www.aseta.es/index_i.htm
www.drive-alive.co.uk/distances.htm
www.drive-alive.co.uk/autoroutes.htm

▼ **Country identification**

- **AND** Andorra
- **E** Spain
- **F** France
- **GBZ** Gibraltar
- **MA** Morocco
- **P** Portugal

▼ **Tourist information**

Spain
Spanish Tourist Office
2nd Floor
79 New Cavendish Street
London
W1W 6XB

www.spain.info
tel: 020 7486 8077

Portugal
Portuguese Tourism Office
11 Belgrave Square
London
SW1X 8PP

www.portugal.insite.com
tel: 0845 355 1212

Distance chart

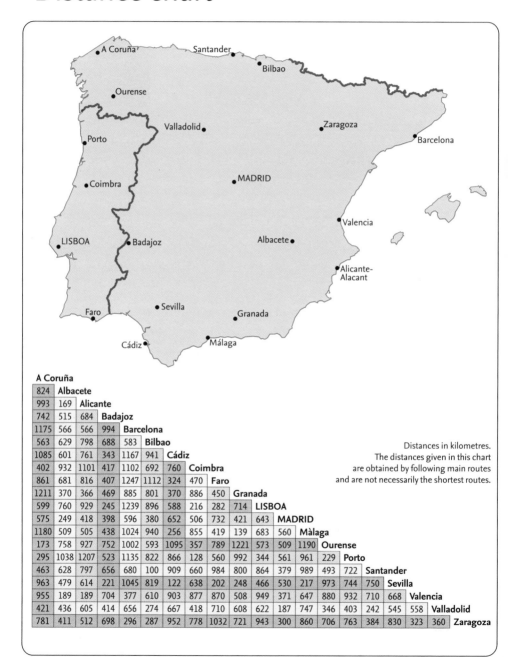

Distances in kilometres.
The distances given in this chart
are obtained by following main routes
and are not necessarily the shortest routes.

A Coruña

824	**Albacete**																		
993	169	**Alicante**																	
742	515	684	**Badajoz**																
1175	566	566	994	**Barcelona**															
563	629	798	688	583	**Bilbao**														
1085	601	761	343	1167	941	**Cádiz**													
402	932	1101	417	1102	692	760	**Coimbra**												
861	681	816	407	1247	1112	324	470	**Faro**											
1211	370	366	469	885	801	370	886	450	**Granada**										
599	760	929	245	1239	896	588	216	282	714	**LISBOA**									
575	249	418	398	596	380	652	506	732	421	643	**MADRID**								
1180	509	505	438	1024	940	256	855	419	139	683	560	**Màlaga**							
173	758	927	752	1002	593	1095	357	789	1221	573	509	1190	**Ourense**						
295	1038	1207	523	1135	822	866	128	560	992	344	561	961	229	**Porto**					
463	628	797	656	680	100	909	660	984	800	864	379	989	493	722	**Santander**				
963	479	614	221	1045	819	122	638	202	248	466	530	217	973	744	750	**Sevilla**			
955	189	189	704	377	610	903	877	870	508	949	371	647	880	932	710	668	**Valencia**		
421	436	605	414	656	274	667	418	710	608	622	187	747	346	403	242	545	558	**Valladolid**	
781	411	512	698	296	287	952	778	1032	721	943	300	860	706	763	384	830	323	360	**Zaragoza**

Key to map pages

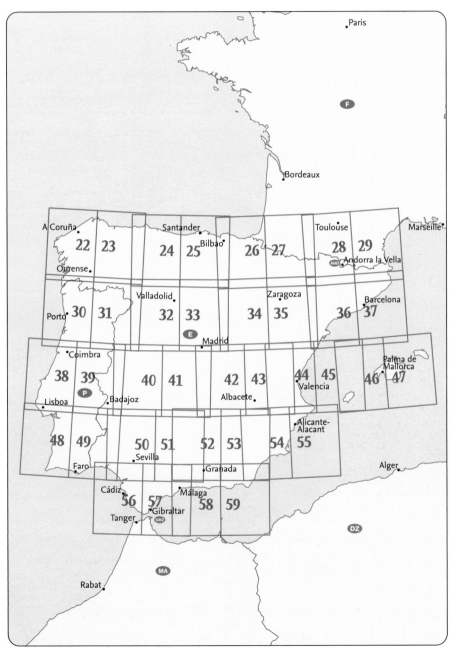

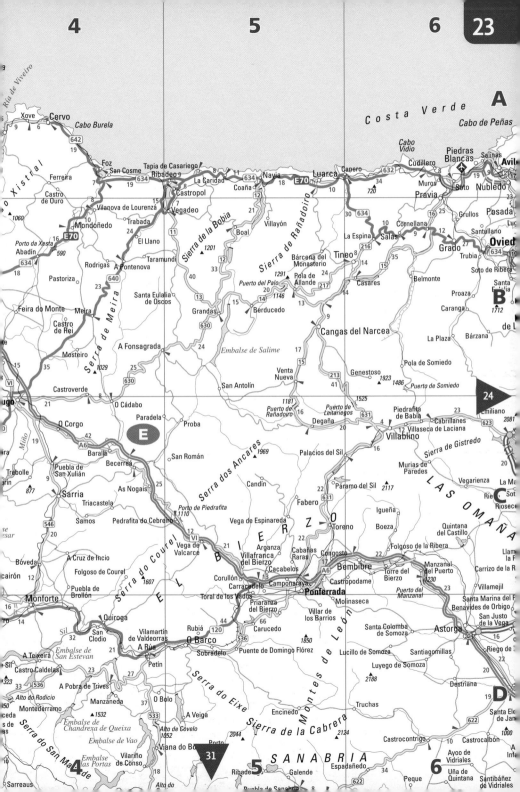

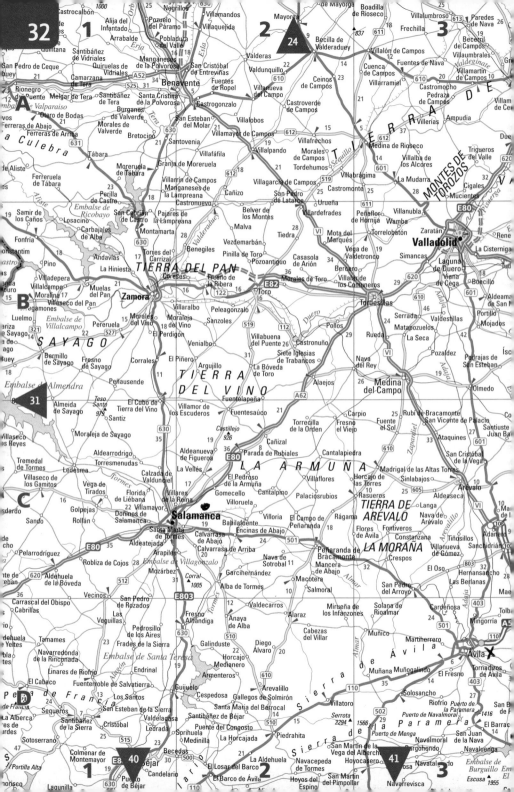

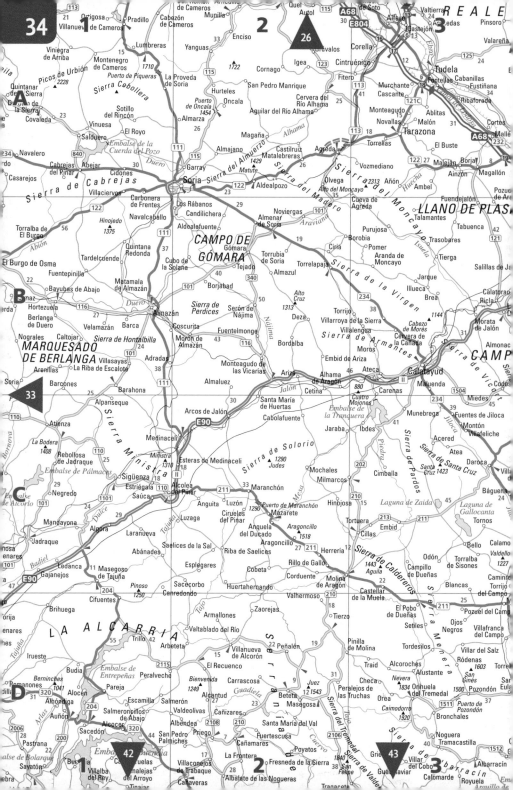

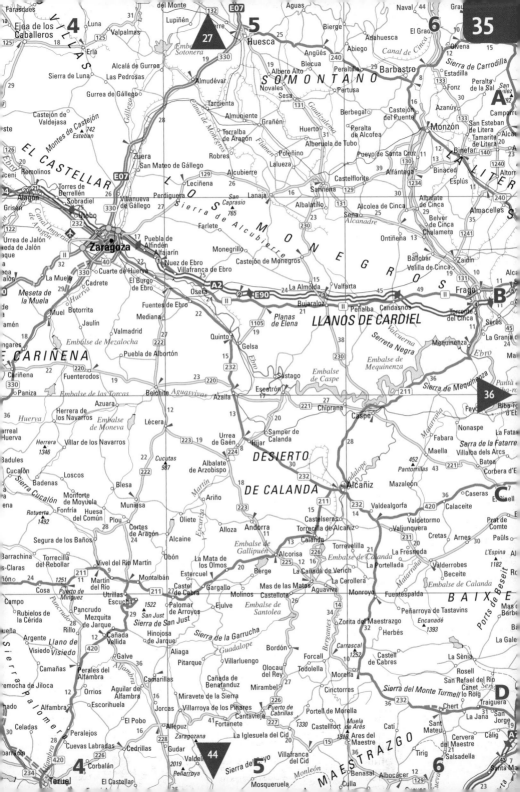

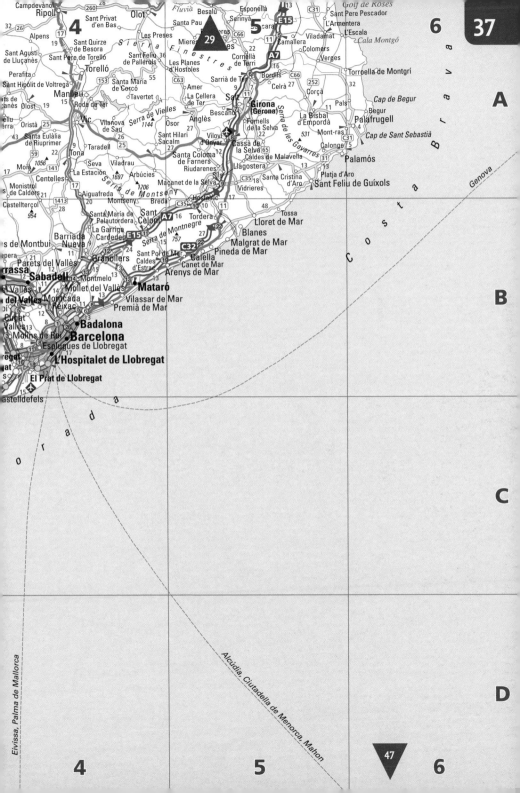

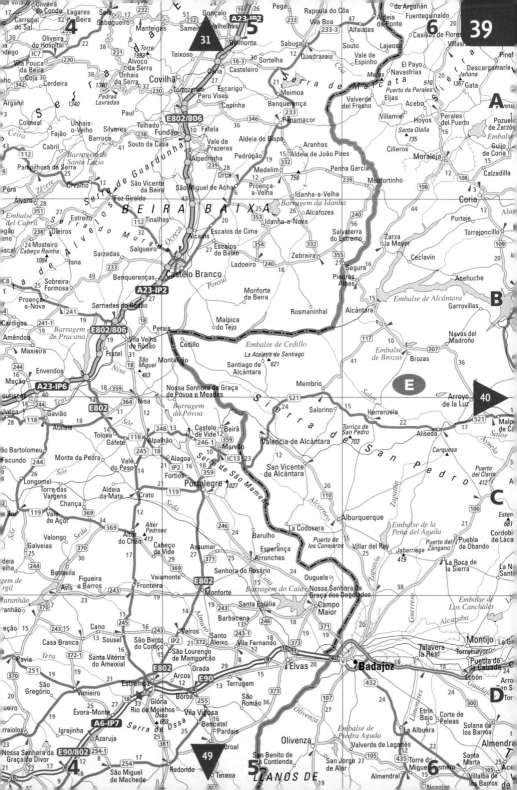

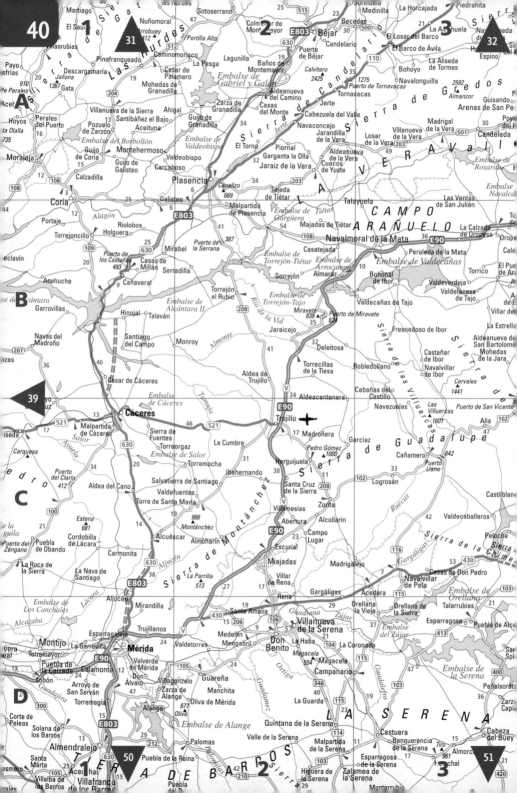

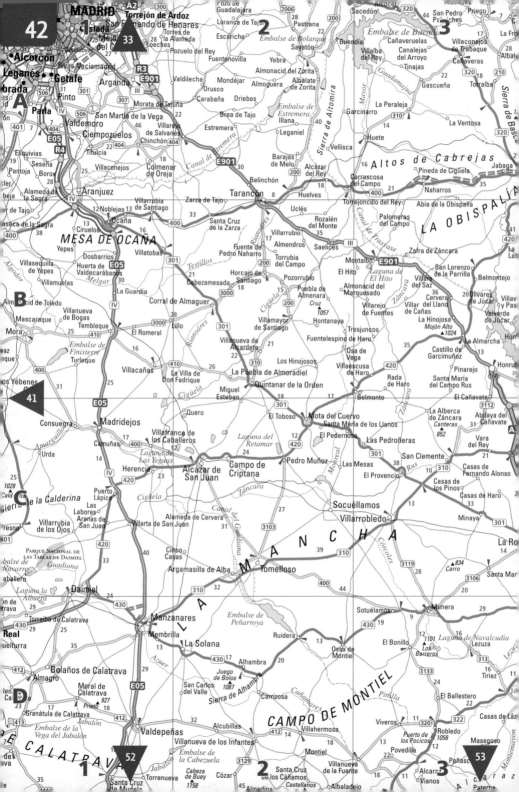

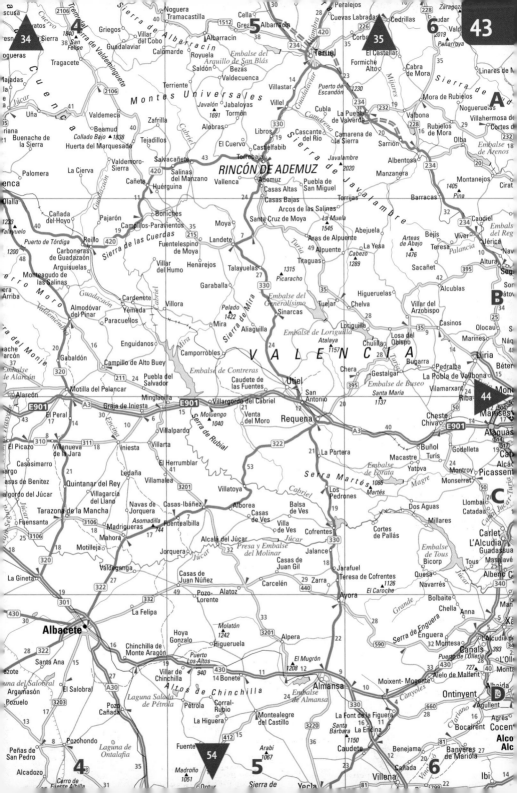

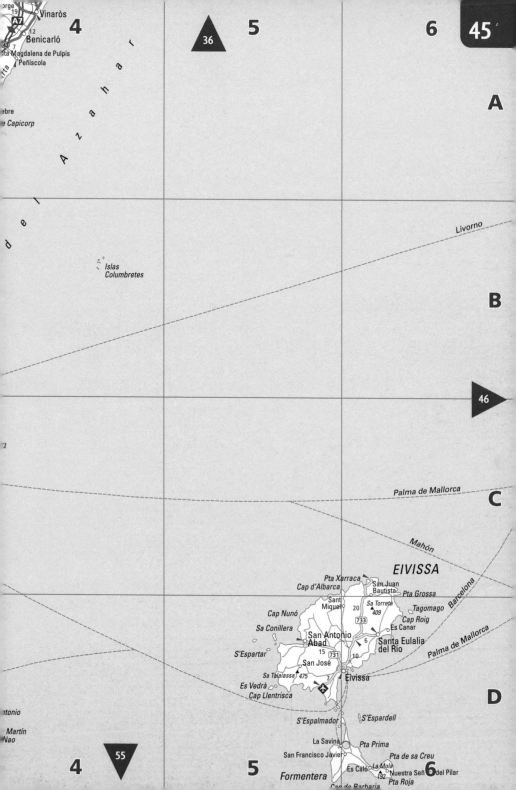

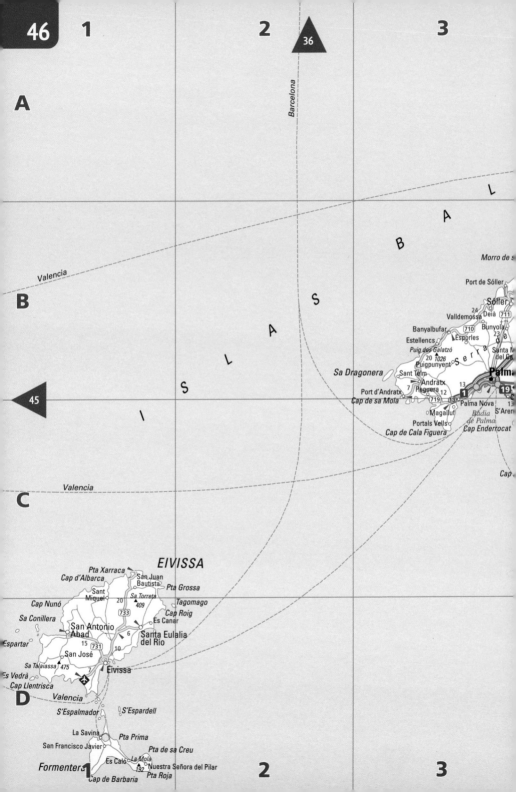

A

1

2

3

36

Barcelona

Valencia

B

Morro de s

Port de Sóller

Sóller

Valldemossa · Deià · 711

Banyalbufar · 24 · 710 · Bunyola · 23

Estellencs · Esporles · Santa M

Puig des Galatzó · 1026 · del G

20 · Puigpunyent · Serra

Sa Dragonera · Sant Telm

Andratx · 13 · Palma

45 · Peguera · 12 · 1 · 19

Port d'Andratx · 7 · 719 · 13 · Palma Nova

Cap de sa Mola · 13 · S'Aren

Magaluf · Badia

Portals Vells · de Palma

Cap de Cala Figuera · Cap Enderrocat

Cap

Valencia

C

EIVISSA

Pta Xarraca

Cap d'Albarca · San Juan Bautista

Pta Grossa

Cap Nunó · Sant Miquel · 20 · Sa Torreta · Tagomago

409

733 · Cap Roig

Sa Conillera · Es Canar

San Antonio Abad · 6 · Santa Eulalia del Río

Espartar · 15 · 731

San José · 10

Sa Talaiassa · 475 · 7

Es Vedrà · Eivissa

Cap Llentrisca

D

Valencia

S'Espardell

S'Espalmador

La Savina · Pta Prima

San Francisco Javier · Pta de sa Creu

Es Caló · La Mola · Nuestra Señora del Pilar

Formentera · 132 · Pta Roja

Cap de Barbaria

1

2

3

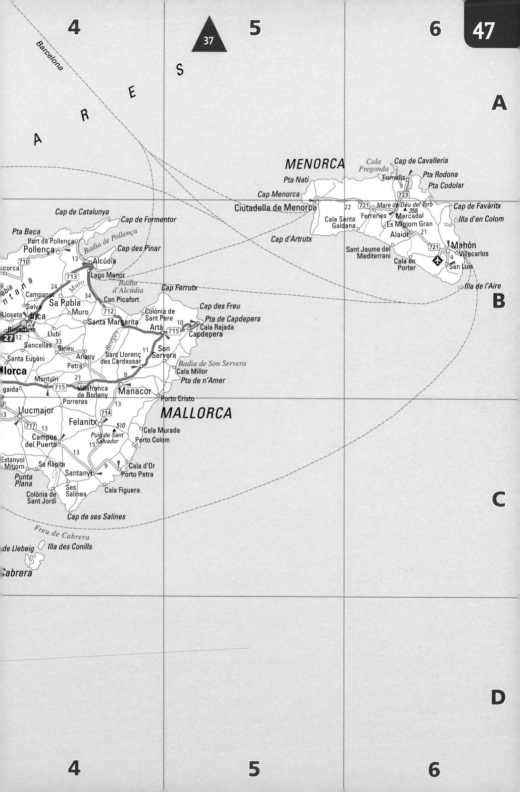

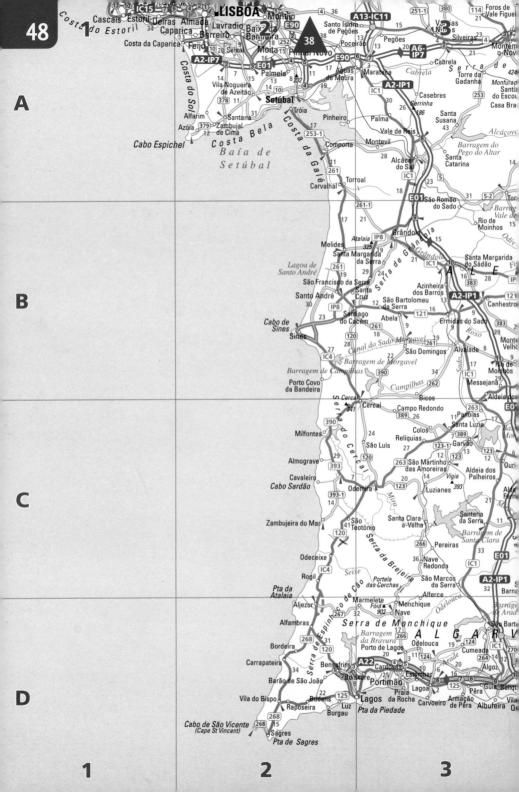

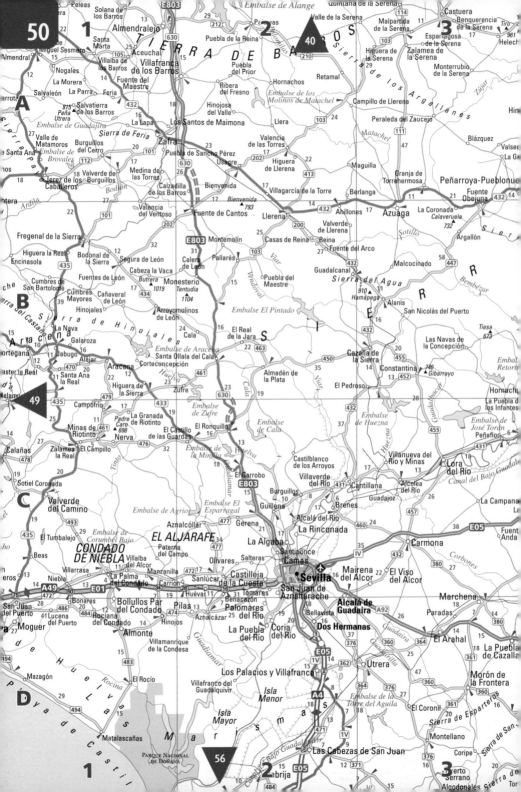

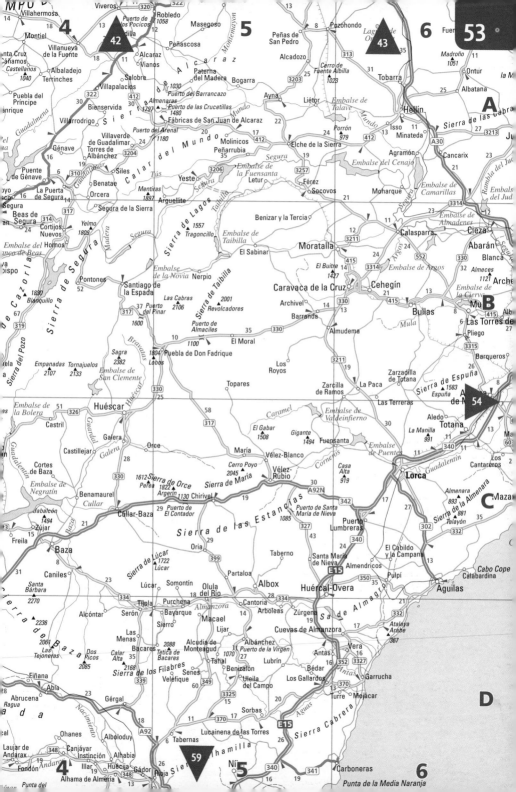

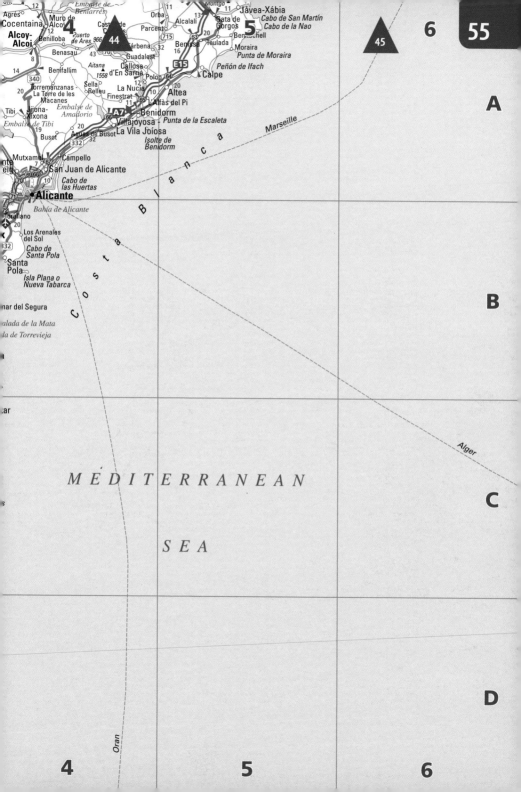

Embalse de Benarrés

Agrés Cocentaina Muro de Orba **11** Mongó **11** Jávea-Xábia
Alcoy- Alcoi Benilloba Castell de Parcent Alcalali Cabo de San Martín **5**
44 Puerto de Ares Cabo de la Nao
Benasau **43** **966** Càrbena Teulada Benitachell
Benifallim Guadalest **16** Benissa **63** Moraira
Aitana Callosa Punta de Moraira
14 **1558** d'En Sarrià Peñón de Ifach
Sella Polop Calpe
Torremanzanas Relleu **12**
La Torre de les Finestrat **10** L'Alfàs del Pi
Macanes Altea
Tibi Jijona- La Nucia **A**
Xixona Embalse de La Nucia
Embalse de Tibi Amadorio **A7** Benidorm
Busot **66** Villajoyosa Punta de la Escaleta
332 Aguas de Busot La Vila Joiosa
Mutxamel **7** Campello Isolte de
San Juan de Alicante Benidorm
eig **69 68** Cabo de
70 **10** las Huertas

Alicante

Torellano Bahía de Alicante
20
Los Arenales del Sol
332 Cabo de
Santa Pola
Santa Pola Isla Plana o **B**
Nueva Tabarca

mar del Segura
alada de la Mata
a de Torrevieja

Marseille

Costa Blanca

Alger

M E D I T E R R A N E A N **C**

S E A

Oran **D**

4 **5** **6**

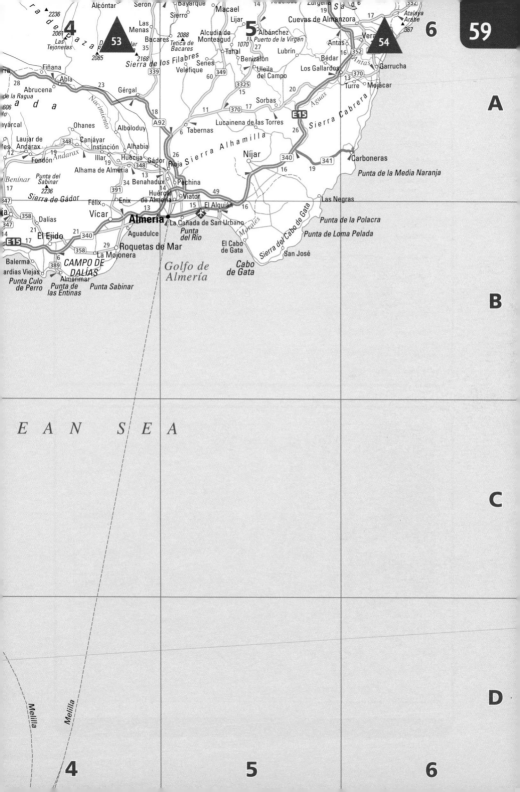

Alcóntar · Seron · Bayarque · Macael · 14 · Arboleas · Zurgena · S a d e 19
Las Menas · Sierro · Líjar · Cuevas de Almanzora · Atalaya Árabe · 17 367
2236 · 2061 · 53 · Bacares · 2088 · Alcudia de Monteagud · Albánchez · Antas · Vera · 54 · 6
Las Tejoneras · D · 35 · Tetica de Bacares · Puerto de la Virgen · Bédar · 16 · 352
2085 · 2168 · Sierra de los Filabres · 1070 · 27 · Tahal · Lubrín · Los Gallardos · Garrucha
Fiñana · 339 · Senes · Benizalón · Uleila del Campo · 13 · 370 · Turre · Mojácar
28 · Abrucena · Abla · 23 · Gérgal · Velefique · 60 · 349 · 3325 · 20 · 370
de la Ragua · 606 · Ohanes · 18 · 11 · 370 · 15 · Sorbas · 26 · Sierra Cabrera
a · d · a · Alboloduy · A92 · 17 · Lucainena de las Torres · E15 · Aguas
Laujar de Andarax · 348 · Canjáyar · Instinción · 6 · Tabernas · Sierra Alhamilla · 26
12 · 19 · Illar · Alhabia · 26 · Níjar · 340 · 341 · Carboneras
Fondón · Andarax · 19 · Huécija · 348 · Gádor · Rioja · 16 · 19 · Punta de la Media Naranja
Benínar · Punta del Sabinar · Alhama de Almería · 13 · Pechina · 49
17 · 2236 · 391 · 34 · Benahadux · Huércal de Almería · Viator · Las Negras
347 · Félix · Sierra de Gádor · Enix · 13 · 15 · El Alquián · 16
1a · 358 · Vícar · Almería · La Cañada de San Urbano · Punta de la Polacra
14 · Dalías · 21 · Aguadulce · Punta del Río · Punta de Loma Pelada
E15 · El Ejido · 340 · 17 · La Mojonera · El Cabo de Gata · San José
358 · 29 · Roquetas de Mar · Golfo de Almería · Cabo de Gata
Balerma · 6 · CAMPO DE DALÍAS · Sierra del Cabo de Gata
ardias Viejas · 389 · Almerimar
347 · Punta Culo de Perro · Punta de las Entinas · Punta Sabinar

E A N   S E A

Melilla · Melilla

Key to city map symbols

E55	Euro route number
A13	Motorway
	Motorway – toll
17	Motorway junction – full access
12	Motorway junction – restricted access
	Motorway services
309	Main road – dual carriageway
	Main road – single carriageway
516	Secondary road – dual carriageway
	Secondary road – single carriageway
	Other road
	Motorway tunnel
	Main road tunnel
	Motorway/road under construction
	Road toll

✈	International airport
	Railway
	Tunnel
	Funicular railway
	Car ferry
▲480	Summit (height in metres)
	Canal
	International boundary
	Urban area
	Parkland
	Woodland
★	Place of interest

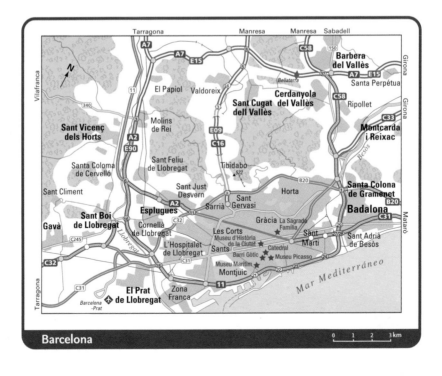

Barcelona

0 1 2 3 km

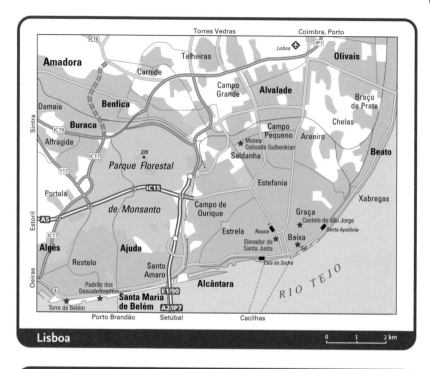

Lisboa

0　1　2 km

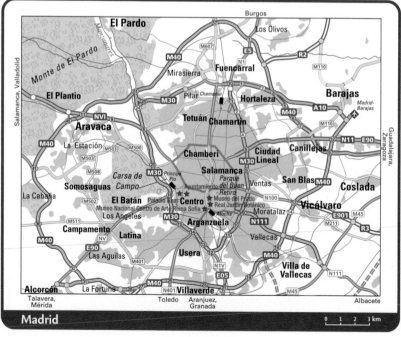

Madrid

0　1　2　3 km

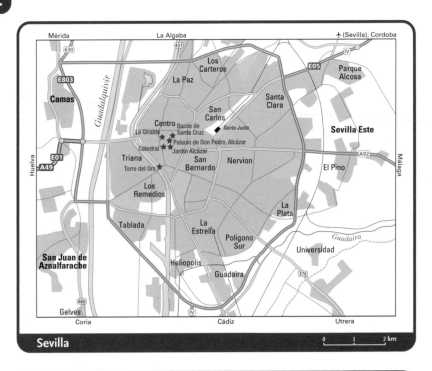

Sevilla

0 1 2 km

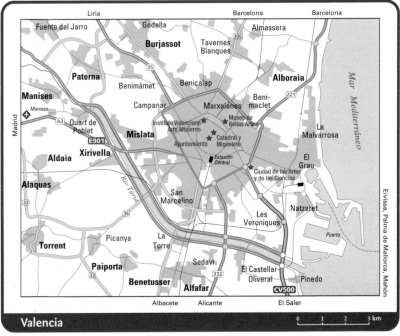

Valencia

0 1 2 3 km

A

A Armada *E* **22** B3
Abades *E* **33** C4
Abadín *E* **23** B4
Abadiño *E* **26** B1
A Baiuca *E* **22** B2
Abánades *E* **34** C1
Abanilla *E* **54** B3
Abarán *E* **53** B6
A Barrela *E* **22** D3
Abejar *E* **33** A6
Abejuela *E* **43** B6
Abela *P* **48** B3
Abenójar *E* **41** D5
Abertura *E* **40** C2
Abia de la Obispalía *E* **42** B3
Abiego *E* **27** D6
Abla *E* **53** D4
Ablitas *E* **34** A3
Abragão *P* **30** C3
Abrantes *P* **38** C3
Abreiro *P* **31** B4
Abrigada *P* **38** C2
Abrucena *E* **53** D4
A Cañiza *E* **22** D2
A Carballa *E* **22** B1
A Carreira *E* **22** B3
Acebo *E* **39** A6
Acedera *E* **40** C3
Acedo *E* **26** C2
Acehuche *E* **39** B6
Aceituna *E* **40** A1
Acered *E* **34** C3
Aceuchal *E* **39** D6
A Chan *E* **22** D2
A Coruña *E* **22** B2
A Cruz de Incio *E* **23** C4
Adahuesca *E* **27** D6
Adamuz *E* **51** B5
Adanero *E* **32** C3
Adão *P* **31** D4
Adaúfe *P* **30** B2
Ademuz *E* **43** A5
Adoufe *P* **30** B3
Adra *E* **59** B4
Adradas *E* **34** B1
Adrados *E* **33** B4
Adzaneta *E* **44** A3
Adzaneta de Albaida *E* **43** D6
A Escusa *E* **22** D2
A Esfarrapada *E* **22** D2
A Estrada *E* **22** C2
Afife *P* **30** A1
A Fonsagrada *E* **23** B4
A Forxa *E* **22** D3
A Forxa *E* **30** A3
Agallas *E* **31** D6
A Gándara *E* **22** C3
A Gándara de Altea *E* **22** A3
Àger *E* **28** D1
Agolada *E* **22** C3
Agoncillo *E* **26** D2
Agost *E* **54** A3

Agramón *E* **53** A6
Agramunt *E* **36** A2
Agreda *E* **34** A2
Agrés *E* **43** D6
Agrochão *P* **31** B5
Aguadulce *E* **51** D4
Aguadulce *E* **59** B4
A Guarda *E* **30** A1
Aguarón *E* **35** B4
Aguas *E* **27** D5
Águas Belas *P* **38** B3
Aguas de Busot *E* **55** A4
Águas de Moura *P* **38** D2
Águas Frias *P* **31** A4
Aguaviva *E* **35** C5
A Gudiña *E* **31** A4
Agudo *E* **41** D4
Águeda *P* **30** D2
Aguiar *P* **49** A4
Aguiar da Beira *P* **31** C4
Aguilafuente *E* **33** C4
Aguilar de Alfambra *E* **35** D4
Aguilar de Campóo *E* **25** C4
Aguilar de la Frontera *E* **51** C5
Aguilar del Río Alhama *E* **34** A2
Águilas *E* **53** C6
Agullana *E* **29** D5
Agullent *E* **43** D6
Ahigal *E* **40** A2
Ahigal de Villarino *E* **31** C6
Ahillones *E* **50** B2
Aibar *E* **26** C3
Aielo de Malferit *E* **43** D6
A Igrexa *E* **22** D2
Aiguafreda *E* **37** A4
Ainsa *E* **27** D6
Ainzón *E* **34** A3
Aitona *E* **35** B6
Aizpún *E* **26** C3
Ajo *E* **25** A5
Ajofrín *E* **41** B5
Alaejos *E* **32** B2
A Lagoa *E* **22** D2
Alagoa *P* **39** C5
Alagón *E* **35** A4
Alaior *E* **47** B6
Alájar *E* **49** B6
Alameda *E* **51** D5
Alameda de Cervera *E* **42** C2
Alameda de la Sagra *E* **41** A6
Alamedilla *E* **52** C3
Alamillo *E* **41** D4
Alandroal *P* **39** D5
Alange *E* **40** D1
Alanís *E* **50** B3
Alaquàs *E* **43** C6
Alaraz *E* **32** D2
Alarcón *E* **43** B4
Alar del Rey *E* **25** C4
Alaró *E* **47** B4
Alatoz *E* **43** C5
Albacete *E* **43** D4
Alba de Tormes *E* **32** C2

Albaida *E* **43** D6
Albaladejo *E* **42** D2
Albalate de Arzobispo *E* **35** C5
Albalate de Cinca *E* **35** B6
Albalate de las Nogueras *E* **34** D2
Albalate de Zorita *E* **42** A2
Albalatillo *E* **35** B5
Albánchez *E* **53** D5
Albanyà *E* **29** D5
Albarracín *E* **34** D3
Albatana *E* **53** A6
Albatàrrec *E* **36** B1
Albatera *E* **54** B3
Albelda *E* **35** A6
Albelda de Iregua *E* **26** D2
Albella *E* **27** D6
Albendea *E* **34** D2
Albendín *E* **51** C5
Albentosa *E* **43** A6
Albergaria-a-Velha *P* **30** D2
Albergaria dos Doze *P* **38** B3
Alberic *E* **43** C6
Albernoa *P* **49** B4
Albero Alto *E* **27** D5
Alberuela de Tubo *E* **35** A5
Albesa *E* **36** A1
Albires *E* **24** D2
Albocàcer *E* **35** D6
Alboloduy *E* **53** D4
Albolote *E* **51** D6
Albondón *E* **58** B3
Alboraya *E* **44** C2
Alborea *E* **43** C5
Albox *E* **53** C5
Albudeite *E* **53** B6
Albufeira *P* **48** D3
Albujón *E* **54** C3
Albuñol *E* **58** B3
Albuñuelas *E* **51** D6
Alburquerque *E* **39** C5
Alcácer *E* **44** C2
Alcácer do Sal *P* **48** A3
Alcáçovas *P* **48** A3
Alcadozo *E* **43** D4
Alcafozes *P* **39** B5
Alcaine *E* **35** C5
Alcains *P* **39** B5
Alcalá de Chivert *E* **44** A3
Alcalá de Guadaira *E* **50** D2
Alcalá de Gurrea *E* **27** D5
Alcalá de Henares *E* **33** D5
Alcalá del Júcar *E* **43** C5
Alcalá de los Gazules *E* **56** B3
Alcalá del Río *E* **50** C2
Alcalá del Valle *E* **51** D4
Alcalá la Real *E* **51** C6
Alcalalí *E* **44** D3
Alcampell *E* **35** A6
Alcanadre *E* **26** D2
Alcanede *P* **38** C2
Alcanena *E* **38** C3
Alcanhões *P* **38** C3

Alcañices *E* **31** B6
Alcañiz *E* **35** C5
Alcántara *E* **39** B6
Alcantarilla *E* **54** B2
Alcantud *E* **34** D2
Alcaracejos *E* **51** A4
Alcaraz *E* **42** D3
Alcaria Ruiva *P* **49** C4
Alcarràs *E* **36** B1
Alcaucín *E* **51** D6
Alcaudete *E* **51** C6
Alcaudete de la Jara *E* **41** B4
Alcázar del Rey *E* **42** A2
Alcázar de San Juan *E* **42** C2
Alcira *E* **44** C2
Alcoba *E* **41** C5
Alcobaça *P* **38** B2
Alcobendas *E* **33** D5
Alcocer *E* **34** D1
Alcocero de Mola *E* **25** D5
Alcochete *P* **38** D2
Alcoentre *P* **38** C2
Alcolea *E* **51** B5
Alcolea *E* **53** D4
Alcolea de Calatrava *E* **41** D5
Alcolea de Cinca *E* **35** B6
Alcolea del Pinar *E* **34** C1
Alcolea del Río *E* **50** C3
Alcollarín *E* **40** C2
Alconchel *E* **49** A5
Alcóntar *E* **53** D4
Alcora *E* **44** A3
Alcorcón *E* **33** D5
Alcorisa *E* **35** C5
Alcoroches *E* **34** D3
Alcossebre *E* **44** A3
Alcoutim *P* **49** C5
Alcover *E* **36** C2
Alcoy-Alcoi *E* **44** D2
Alcubierre *E* **35** A5
Alcubilla de Avellaneda *E* **33** A6
Alcubillas *E* **42** D2
Alcublas *E* **43** B6
Alcúdia *E* **47** B4
Alcudia de Guadix *E* **52** D3
Alcudia de Monteagud *E* **53** D5
Alcuéscar *E* **40** C1
Aldeacentenera *E* **40** C2
Aldeadávila de la Ribera *E* **31** C5
Aldea del Cano *E* **40** C1
Aldea del Fresno *E* **33** D4
Aldea del Obispo *E* **31** D5
Aldea del Rey *E* **41** D6
Aldea de Trujillo *E* **40** B2
Aldealafuente *E* **34** B2
Aldealpozo *E* **34** A2
Aldeamayor de San Martín *E* **32** B3
Aldeanueva de Barbarroya *E* **41** B4
Aldeanueva de Ebro *E* **26** D2

Aldeanueva de Figueroa *E* 32 C2
Aldeanueva de la Vera *E* 40 A2
Aldeanueva del Camino *E* 40 A2
Aldeanueva de San Bartolomé *E* 40 B3
Aldeaquemada *E* 52 A3
Aldea Real *E* 33 C4
Aldearrodrigo *E* 32 C1
Aldeaseca *E* 32 C3
Aldeatejada *E* 32 C1
Aldeavieja *E* 33 D4
Aldehuela de la Bóveda *E* 31 C6
Aldehuela de Yeltes *E* 31 D6
Aldeia da Mata *P* 39 C4
Aldeia da Ponte *P* 31 D5
Aldeia de Ferreira *P* 49 A5
Aldeia de João Pires *P* 39 A5
Aldeia do Bispo *P* 39 A5
Aldeia dos Elvas *P* 48 B3
Aldeia dos Fernandes *P* 48 C3
Aldeia dos Palheiros *P* 48 C3
Aldeia Velha *P* 39 C4
Aldover *E* 36 C1
Aledo *E* 53 C6
Alenquer *P* 38 C2
Alerre *E* 27 D5
Alesón *E* 25 D6
Alfacar *E* 52 D2
Alfafar *E* 44 C2
Alfaiates *P* 31 D5
Alfajarín *E* 35 B4
Alfambra *E* 35 D4
Alfambras *P* 48 D2
Alfamén *E* 35 B4
Alfândega da Fé *P* 31 B5
Alfántega *E* 35 A6
Alfarim *P* 48 A2
Alfaro *E* 26 D3
Alfarràs *E* 36 A1
Alfeizerão *P* 38 C2
Alfena *P* 30 C2
Alferce *P* 48 D3
Alforja *E* 36 C2
Alfundão *P* 49 B4
Algaida *P* 47 B4
Algámitas *E* 51 D4
Algar *E* 56 B3
Algarinejo *E* 51 D5
Algarrobo *E* 57 B6
Algatocín *E* 57 B4
Algeciras *E* 57 C4
Algemesí *E* 44 C2
Algerri *E* 36 A1
Algete *E* 33 D5
Alginet *E* 43 C6
Algodonales *E* 50 D3
Algodor *P* 49 C4
Algora *E* 34 C1
Algorta *E* 25 B6
Algoso *P* 31 B5

Algoz *P* 48 D3
Alguaire *E* 36 B1
Alguazas *E* 54 B2
Algueirão-Mem Martins *P* 38 D1
Algueña *E* 54 B3
Alhabia *E* 53 D4
Alhama de Almería *E* 53 D4
Alhama de Aragón *E* 34 B2
Alhama de Granada *E* 51 D6
Alhama de Murcia *E* 53 B6
Alhambra *E* 42 D2
Alhaurín de la Torre *E* 57 B5
Alhaurín el Grande *E* 57 B5
Alhendín *E* 51 D6
Alhóndiga *E* 33 D6
Alía *E* 40 C3
Aliaga *E* 35 D5
Aliaguilla *E* 43 B5
Alicante *E* 55 A4
Alicún de Ortega *E* 52 C3
Alija del Infantado *E* 24 D1
Alijó *P* 31 B4
Aliseda *E* 39 C6
Aljaraque *E* 49 D6
Aljezur *P* 48 D2
Aljubarrota *P* 38 B2
Aljucén *E* 40 C1
Aljustrel *P* 48 B3
Allariz *E* 22 D3
Allepuz *E* 35 D4
Allo *E* 26 C2
Alloza *E* 35 C5
Almacelles *E* 35 B6
Almáchar *E* 57 B6
Almada *P* 38 D2
Almadén *E* 41 D4
Almadén de la Plata *E* 50 B2
Almadenejos *E* 41 D4
Almagro *E* 41 D6
Almajano *E* 34 A2
Almalaguês *P* 38 A3
Almaluez *E* 34 B2
Almansa *E* 43 D5
Almansil *P* 49 D4
Almanza *E* 24 C3
Almaraz *E* 40 B2
Almargen *E* 51 D4
Almarza *E* 34 A2
Almassora *E* 44 B3
Almazán *E* 34 B1
Almazora *E* 44 B3
Almazul *E* 34 B2
Almedina *E* 42 D2
Almedinilla *E* 51 C6
Almeida de Sayago *E* 31 B6
Almeirim *P* 38 C3
Almenar *E* 36 A1
Almenara *E* 44 B3
Almenar de Soria *E* 34 B2
Almendra *E* 31 C6
Almendra *P* 31 C5
Almendral *E* 39 D6
Almendralejo *E* 40 D1
Almendricos *E* 53 C6

Almendros *E* 42 B2
Almería *E* 59 B5
Almerimar *E* 59 B4
Almodóvar *P* 49 C4
Almodóvar del Campo *E* 41 D5
Almodóvar del Pinar *E* 43 B4
Almodóvar del Río *E* 51 C4
Almofala *P* 30 C3
Almogía *E* 57 B6
Almograve *P* 48 C2
Almoguera *E* 42 A2
Almoharín *E* 40 C2
Almonacid de la Sierra *E* 34 B3
Almonacid del Marquesado *E* 42 B2
Almonacid del Zorita *E* 33 D6
Almonacid de Toledo *E* 41 B6
Almonaster la Real *E* 49 B6
Almonte *E* 49 D6
Almoradí *E* 54 B3
Almorchón *E* 40 D3
Almorox *E* 41 A5
Almoster *P* 38 B3
Almudema *E* 53 B5
Almudévar *E* 27 D5
Almuñécar *E* 58 B2
Almuniente *E* 35 A5
Álmuradiel *E* 52 A3
Almussafes *E* 44 C2
Alobras *E* 43 A5
Alocén *E* 34 D1
Álora *E* 57 B5
Alós d'Ensil *E* 28 C2
Alosno *E* 49 C5
Alovera *E* 33 D6
Alozaina *E* 57 B5
Alp *E* 28 D3
Alpalhão *P* 39 C4
Alpanseque *E* 34 C1
Alpedrinha *P* 39 A5
Alpedriz *P* 38 B2
Alpens *E* 29 D4
Alpera *E* 43 D5
Alpiarça *P* 38 C3
Alpuente *E* 43 B5
Alquería de la Condesa *E* 44 D3
Alquerías *E* 54 B3
Alqueva *P* 49 B5
Alquife *E* 52 D3
Altafulla *E* 36 C3
Alte *P* 48 D3
Altea *E* 55 A5
Alter do Chão *P* 39 C4
Altorricón *E* 35 A6
Altsasu *E* 26 C2
Altura *E* 43 B6
Alustante *E* 34 D3
Alvaiázere *P* 38 B3
Alvalade *P* 48 B3
Alvarenga *P* 30 C3

Álvares *P* 39 A4
Álvaro *P* 39 B4
Alvega *P* 39 C4
Alvelos *P* 30 B2
Alverca *P* 38 D2
Alverca da Beira *P* 31 D4
Alvito *P* 49 B4
Alvoco da Serra *P* 39 A4
Alzira *E* 44 C2
Amadora *P* 38 D2
Amaiur-Maia *E* 26 B3
Amarante *P* 30 B3
Amareleja *P* 49 B5
Amares *P* 30 B2
Ambasaguas *E* 24 C2
Ambel *E* 34 A3
Ameixial *P* 49 C4
Amêndoa *P* 39 B4
Amendoeira *P* 49 C4
Amer *E* 29 D5
A Merca *E* 22 D3
Amezketa *E* 26 B2
Amieira *P* 49 A5
Amoeiro *E* 22 D3
Amonde *P* 30 A2
Amorebieta *E* 25 B6
Amposta *E* 36 D1
Ampudia *E* 32 A3
Ampuero *E* 25 B5
Amurrio *E* 25 B6
Amusco *E* 25 D4
Anadia *P* 30 D2
Anaya de Alba *E* 32 D2
Ancín *E* 26 C2
Andavías *E* 32 B1
Andoain *E* 26 B2
Andorra *E* 35 C5
Andorra la Vella *AND* 28 C3
Andosilla *E* 26 D2
Andratx *E* 46 B3
Andújar *E* 51 B6
Angeja *P* 30 D2
Anglès *E* 37 A5
Anglesola *E* 36 B2
Anglesona *E* 36 B2
Angüés *E* 27 D5
Anguiano *E* 25 D6
Anguita *E* 34 C2
Anha *P* 30 B2
Anna *E* 43 D6
Anoeta *E* 26 B2
Añón *E* 34 A3
Añora *E* 51 A4
Añover de Tajo *E* 41 B6
Anquela del Ducado *E* 34 C2
Ansião *P* 38 B3
Ansó *E* 27 C4
Antanhol *P* 38 A3
Antas *E* 53 D6
Antas *P* 30 B2
Antas *P* 31 C4
Antas de Ulla *E* 22 C3
Antequera *E* 51 D5
Antzuola *E* 26 B2
Aoiz *E* 26 C3

Aós *E* **26** C3
A Pedreira *E* **22** D2
A Peroxa *E* **22** D3
A Picota *E* **22** C1
A Pobra de Trives *E* **23** D4
A Pobra do Caramiñal *E* **22** C1
A Pontenova *E* **23** B4
A Pontepedra *E* **22** B2
Aquilué *E* **27** D5
Aracena *E* **49** B6
Aragoncillo *E* **34** C2
Araia *E* **26** C2
A Ramallosa *E* **22** C2
Aranda de Duero *E* **33** B5
Aranda de Moncayo *E* **34** B3
Aranhas *P* **39** A5
Aranjuez *E* **41** A6
Arano *E* **26** B3
Aranzueque *E* **33** D6
Arapiles *E* **32** C2
Aras *E* **26** C2
Aras de Alpuente *E* **43** B5
Arazede *P* **38** A3
Arbeca *E* **36** B2
Arbeteta *E* **34** D2
Arboleas *E* **53** D5
Arbúcies *E* **37** A4
Arceniega *E* **25** B6
Archena *E* **54** B2
Archidona *E* **51** D5
Archivel *E* **53** B5
Arco de Baúlhe *P* **30** B3
Arcos *E* **25** D5
Arcos *P* **39** D5
Arcos de Jalón *E* **34** C2
Arcos de la Frontera *E* **56** B3
Arcos de las Salinas *E* **43** B5
Arcos de Valdevez *P* **30** A2
Arcozelo *P* **30** A2
Arcozelo *P* **30** B2
Arcusa *E* **27** D6
Ardales *E* **57** A5
Ardanaz *E* **26** C3
Areatza *E* **25** B6
Areias *P* **38** B3
Arén *E* **28** D1
Arenas de Iguña *E* **25** B4
Arenas del Rey *E* **51** D6
Arenas de San Juan *E* **41** C6
Arenas de San Pedro *E* **40** A3
Arenillas *E* **33** B6
Arenys de Mar *E* **37** B5
Areosa *P* **30** B1
Ares *E* **22** B3
Ares del Maestre *E* **35** D6
Arespalditza *E* **25** B6
Aretxabaleta *E* **26** B2
Arevalillo *E* **32** D2
Arévalo *E* **32** C3
Argallón *E* **50** B3
Argamasilla de Alba *E* **42** C2
Argamasilla de Calatrava *E* **41** D5
Argamasón *E* **43** D4

Arganda *E* **41** A6
Arganil *P* **39** A4
Arganza *E* **23** C5
Argelita *E* **44** A2
Argente *E* **35** D4
Argés *E* **41** B5
Arguedas *E* **26** D3
Arguellite *E* **53** A5
Arguís *E* **27** D5
Arguisuelas *E* **43** B4
Argujillo *E* **32** B2
Ariany *E* **47** B4
Aribe *E* **27** C4
Arija *E* **25** B4
Ariño *E* **35** C5
Arinsal *AND* **28** C3
Ariz *P* **31** C4
Ariza *E* **34** B2
Arizgoiti *E* **25** B6
Arizola *E* **26** C2
Arjona *E* **51** B6
Arjonilla *E* **51** B6
Arlanzón *E* **25** D5
Armação de Pêra *P* **48** D3
Armallones *E* **34** D2
Armamar *P* **30** C3
Armenteros *E* **32** D2
Armilla *E* **51** D6
Armuña *E* **33** C4
Armunia *E* **24** C2
Arnedillo *E* **26** D2
Arnedo *E* **26** D2
Arnes *E* **35** C6
Arosa *P* **30** B3
Arouca *P* **30** C3
Arquillos *E* **52** B3
Arrabalde *E* **23** D6
Arraia-Maeztu *E* **26** C2
Arraiolos *P* **39** D4
Arranhó *P* **38** D2
Arredondo *E* **25** B5
Arriate *E* **57** B4
Arrifana *P* **31** D4
Arrigorriaga *E* **25** B6
Arriondas *E* **24** B2
Arroba de los Montes *E* **41** C4
Arronches *P* **39** C5
Arroniz *E* **26** C2
Arroyal *E* **25** C4
Arroyo de la Luz *E* **39** C6
Arroyo del Ojanco *E* **53** A4
Arroyo de San Serván *E* **39** D6
Arroyomolinos de León *E* **50** B1
Arruda dos Vinhos *P* **38** D2
Artà *E* **47** B4
Artajona *E* **26** C3
Artana *E* **44** B3
Artés *E* **36** A3
Artesa de Segre *E* **36** A2
Artieda *E* **27** C4
A Rúa *E* **23** D4
Arzúa *E* **22** C3

Ascó *E* **36** C1
As Covas *E* **22** D2
A Serra de Outes *E* **22** C1
Asín *E* **27** D4
As Neves *E* **22** B3
As Neves *E* **22** D2
As Nogais *E* **23** C4
Aspe *E* **54** A3
As Pontes de García Rodríguez *E* **22** B3
Asseiceira *P* **38** C3
Assumar *P* **39** C5
Astorga *E* **23** D6
Astudillo *E* **25** D4
Atalaia *E* **38** C3
Atalaia *P* **39** C4
Atalaya del Cañavate *E* **42** C3
Ataquines *E* **32** C3
Atarfe *E* **51** D6
Atea *E* **34** C3
Ateca *E* **34** B3
A Teixeira *E* **23** D4
Atienza *E* **33** C6
Atouguia da Baleia *P* **38** C1
Auñón *E* **33** D6
Auritz *E* **26** B3
Ausejo *E* **26** D2
Autol *E* **26** D2
Avanca *P* **30** C2
A Veiga *E* **23** D5
Aveiras de Cima *P* **38** C2
Aveiro *P* **30** D2
Avelar *P* **38** B3
Avelãs de Caminho *P* **30** D2
Aveleda *P* **30** B2
Aveleda *P* **31** A5
Avenida do Marqués de Figueroa *E* **22** A3
Avià *E* **28** D3
Ávila *E* **32** D3
A Vila da Igrexa *E* **22** A3
Avilés *E* **23** A6
Avintes *P* **30** C2
Avinyó *E* **37** A4
Avis *P* **39** C4
Ayamonte *E* **49** D5
Ayerbe *E* **27** D5
Ayllón *E* **33** B5
Ayna *E* **53** A5
Ayoo de Vidriales *E* **23** D6
Ayora *E* **43** D5
Azagra *E* **26** D3
Azaila *E* **35** B5
Azambuja *P* **38** C2
Azanúy *E* **35** A6
Azaruja *P* **39** D4
Azcoitia *E* **26** B2
Azinhaga *P* **38** C3
Azinhal *P* **49** D5
Azinheira dos Barros *P* **48** B3
Azinhoso *P* **31** B5
Azkoitia *E* **26** B2
Aznalcázar *E* **50** D2

Aznalcóllar *E* **50** C2
Azóia *P* **48** A2
Azpeitia *E* **26** B2
Azuaga *E* **50** B3
Azuara *E* **35** C4
Azuel *E* **51** A5
Azuelo *E* **26** C2
Azuqueca de Henares *E* **33** D6
Azután *E* **40** B3

B

Babilafuente *E* **32** C2
Bacares *E* **53** D5
Badajoz *E* **39** D6
Badalona *E* **37** B4
Bádames *E* **25** B5
Badarán *E* **25** D6
Badenas *E* **35** C4
Badia Gran *E* **46** C3
Badolatosa *E* **51** D5
Badules *E* **35** C4
Baena *E* **51** C5
Baeza *E* **52** B3
Bagà *E* **28** D3
Báguena *E* **34** C3
Bahabón de Esgueva *E* **33** A5
Bahíllo *E* **24** D3
Bailén *E* **51** B6
Bailo *E* **27** C4
Baio *E* **22** B1
Baiona *E* **22** D2
Baixa da Banheira *P* **38** D2
Bakio-Basigo *E* **25** B6
Balaguer *E* **36** A2
Balazote *E* **43** D4
Baleizão *P* **49** B4
Balerma *E* **59** B4
Ballesteros de Calatrava *E* **41** D5
Ballobar *E* **35** B6
Balmaseda *E* **25** B6
Balneario de Panticosa Huesca *E* **27** C5
Balsa de Ves *E* **43** C5
Balsa Pintada *E* **54** C3
Balsareny *E* **36** A3
Balsicas *E* **54** C3
Baltanás *E* **33** A4
Baltar *E* **30** A3
Bande *E* **30** A3
Bañobárez *E* **31** C5
Bañolas *E* **29** D5
Bañón *E* **35** C4
Baños de la Encina *E* **51** B6
Baños de Molgas *E* **22** D3
Baños de Montemayor *E* **32** D1
Baños de Río Tobía *E* **25** D6
Baños de Valdearados *E* **33** A5
Banyalbufar *E* **46** B3

Banyeres de Mariola *E* 43 D6
Banyoles *E* 29 D5
Baracaldo *E* 25 B6
Barahona *E* 34 B1
Barajas de Melo *E* 42 A2
Barakaldo *E* 25 B6
Baralla *E* 23 C4
Barañain *E* 26 C3
Baranbio *E* 25 B6
Barão de São João *P* 48 D2
Barásoain *E* 26 C3
Barbacena *P* 39 D5
Barbadás *E* 22 D3
Barbadillo de Herreros *E* 25 D6
Barbadillo del Mercado *E* 25 D5
Barbadillo del Pez *E* 25 D6
Barbastro *E* 27 D6
Barbate de Franco *E* 56 C3
Barberá del Vallès *E* 37 B4
Barca *E* 34 B1
Barcabo *E* 27 D6
Barca de Alva *P* 31 C5
Barcarrota *E* 49 A6
Barcelinhos *P* 30 B2
Barcelona *E* 37 B4
Barcelos *P* 30 B2
Bárcena del Monasterio *E* 23 B5
Bárcena de Pie de Concha *E* 25 B4
Barcenillas de Cerezos *E* 25 B5
Barcones *E* 33 B6
Barcos *P* 31 C4
Bárdena *E* 27 D4
Bargas *E* 41 B5
Barinas *E* 54 B3
Barqueros *E* 53 B6
Barquinha *P* 38 C3
Barracas *E* 43 A6
Barrachina *E* 35 C4
Barral *E* 22 D3
Barranco do Velho *P* 49 D4
Barrancos *P* 49 B6
Barranda *E* 53 B5
Barrax *E* 42 D3
Barreiro *P* 38 D2
Barriada Nueva *E* 37 B4
Bárrio *P* 30 A2
Barrio del Peral *E* 54 C3
Barrio Mar *E* 44 B3
Barroca *P* 39 A4
Barroselas *P* 30 B2
Barruecopardo *E* 31 C5
Barruelo de Santullan *E* 25 C4
Barulho *P* 39 C5
Barxeta *E* 44 D2
Bárzana *E* 23 B6
Bàscara *E* 29 D5
Basconcillos del Tozo *E* 25 C4

Batalha *P* 38 B2
Batea *E* 35 C6
Baterno *E* 41 D4
Bayárcal *E* 53 D4
Bayarque *E* 53 D5
Bayona *E* 22 D2
Bayubas de Abajo *E* 33 B6
Baza *E* 53 C4
Beamud *E* 43 A4
Beariz *E* 22 D2
Beas *E* 49 C6
Beasain *E* 26 B2
Beas de Granada *E* 52 D3
Beas de Segura *E* 53 B4
Becedas *E* 32 D2
Beceite *E* 35 C6
Becerreá *E* 23 C4
Becerril de Campos *E* 24 D3
Becilla de Valderaduey *E* 24 D2
Bédar *E* 53 D5
Bedmar *E* 52 C3
Begíjar *E* 52 B3
Begonte *E* 22 B3
Begur *E* 37 A6
Beirã *P* 39 C5
Beja *P* 49 B4
Béjar *E* 32 D1
Bejís *E* 43 B6
Belalcázar *E* 51 A4
Belascoáin *E* 26 C3
Belazaima do Chão *P* 30 D2
Belchite *E* 35 B4
Belianes *E* 36 B2
Belinchón *E* 42 A2
Bellavista *E* 50 D2
Bellclaire d'Urgell *E* 36 A2
Bell-Lloc d'Urgell *E* 36 B2
Bello *E* 34 C3
Bellpuig *E* 36 B2
Bellreguard *E* 44 D3
Bellver de Cerdanya *E* 28 D3
Bélmez *E* 51 B4
Bélmez de la Moraleda *E* 52 C3
Belmonte *E* 23 B6
Belmonte *E* 42 B3
Belmonte *P* 31 D4
Belmontejo *E* 42 B3
Belorado *E* 25 D6
Belver de Cinca *E* 35 B6
Belver de los Montes *E* 32 B2
Belvís de la Jara *E* 41 B4
Bembibre *E* 22 C2
Bembibre *E* 23 C6
Bemposta *P* 31 B5
Bemposta *P* 38 C3
Benabarre *E* 27 D6
Benacazón *E* 50 C2
Benahadux *E* 53 D5
Benahavís *E* 57 B5
Benalmádena *E* 57 B5
Benalúa de Guadix *E* 52 D3
Benalúa de las Villas *E* 51 C6

Benalup de Sidonia *E* 56 C3
Benamargosa *E* 57 B6
Benamaurel *E* 53 C4
Benamejí *E* 51 D5
Benamocarra *E* 57 B6
Benaocaz *E* 57 B4
Benaoján *E* 57 B4
Benasal *E* 35 D6
Benasau *E* 44 D2
Benasque *E* 27 C6
Benatae *E* 53 A4
Benavente *E* 32 A2
Benavente *P* 38 D2
Benavides de Orbigo *E* 23 D6
Benavila *P* 39 C4
Bencatel *P* 39 D5
Benedita *P* 38 C2
Benegiles *E* 32 B2
Benejama *E* 43 D6
Benejúzar *E* 54 B3
Benfica do Ribatejo *P* 38 C3
Benia de Onís *E* 24 B3
Beniarbeig *E* 44 D3
Beniarrés *E* 44 D2
Benicarló *E* 35 D6
Benicasim *E* 44 A3
Benidorm *E* 55 A4
Beniel *E* 54 B3
Benifaió *E* 44 C2
Benifallet *E* 36 C1
Benifallim *E* 44 D2
Benifayo *E* 44 C2
Benigánim *E* 44 D2
Benilloba *E* 44 D2
Benissa *E* 44 D3
Benissanet *E* 36 C1
Benitachell *E* 44 D3
Benizalón *E* 53 D5
Benizar y la Tercia *E* 53 B5
Benlloch *E* 44 A3
Benquerença *P* 39 A5
Benquerenças *P* 39 B4
Benquerencia de la Serena *E* 40 D3
Bensafrim *P* 48 D2
Bera de Bidasoa *E* 26 B3
Beranga *E* 25 B5
Berango *E* 25 B6
Berantevilla *E* 25 C6
Berbegal *E* 35 A6
Bercedo *E* 25 B5
Bercero *E* 32 B3
Bérchules *E* 52 D3
Bercianos del Páramo *E* 24 D1
Berducedo *E* 23 B5
Berdún *E* 27 C4
Berga *E* 28 D3
Bergara *E* 26 B2
Bergasa *E* 26 D2
Berge *E* 35 C5
Beringel *P* 49 B4
Berja *E* 59 B4
Berlanga *E* 50 A2

Berlanga de Duero *E* 33 B6
Bermeo *E* 25 B6
Bermillo de Sayago *E* 31 B6
Bernardos *E* 33 C4
Bernedo *E* 26 C2
Berriatua *E* 26 B2
Berriozar *E* 26 C3
Bertamirans *E* 22 C2
Besalú *E* 29 D5
Besande *E* 24 C3
Bescanó *E* 37 A5
Betanzos *E* 22 B3
Betelu *E* 26 B2
Bétera *E* 43 B6
Beteta *E* 34 D2
Betxí *E* 44 B3
Bezas *E* 43 A5
Biar *E* 43 D6
Bicorp *E* 43 C6
Bicos *P* 48 B3
Biel *E* 27 D4
Bielsa *E* 27 C6
Bienservida *E* 53 A4
Bienvenida *E* 50 A2
Bierge *E* 27 D6
Biescas *E* 27 C5
Bigastro *E* 54 B3
Bigüézal *E* 27 C4
Bilbao *E* 25 B6
Bilbo *E* 25 B6
Binaced *E* 35 A6
Binefar *E* 35 A6
Biniés *E* 27 C4
Binisalem *E* 47 B4
Biosca *E* 36 A2
Biota *E* 27 D4
Biurrun *E* 26 C3
Blanca *E* 53 B6
Blancas *E* 34 C3
Blanes *E* 37 B5
Blázquez *E* 50 A3
Blecua *E* 27 D5
Blesa *E* 35 C4
Blimea *E* 24 B2
Boada *E* 31 C6
Boadilla del Monte *E* 33 D5
Boadilla de Rioseco *E* 24 D3
Boal *E* 23 B5
Boalhosa *P* 30 A2
Boa Vista *P* 38 B2
Boavista *P* 38 C1
Bobadilla *E* 51 D4
Boborás *E* 22 D3
Bocacara *E* 31 D6
Bocairent *E* 43 D6
Boceguillas *E* 33 B5
Bodonal de la Sierra *E* 49 B6
Boecillo *E* 32 B3
Boeza *E* 23 C6
Bogajo *E* 31 C5
Bogarra *E* 53 A5
Bohonal de Ibor *E* 40 B3
Bohoyo *E* 32 D2
Boiro de Arriba *E* 22 C1

Bolaños de Calatrava *E* 41 D6
Bolbaite *E* 43 D6
Bolea *E* 27 D5
Boliqueime *P* 48 D3
Bollullos Par del Condado *E* 49 C6
Boltaña *E* 27 D6
Bombarral *P* 38 C2
Bonanza *E* 56 B2
Boñar *E* 24 C2
Bonares *E* 49 D6
Bonete *E* 43 D5
Boniches *E* 43 B4
Borba *P* 39 D5
Bordalba *E* 34 B2
Bordeira *P* 48 D2
Bordils *E* 29 D5
Bordón *E* 35 D5
Borja *E* 34 A3
Borjabad *E* 34 B2
Bornes *P* 31 B5
Bornes de Aguiar *P* 31 B4
Bornos *E* 56 B3
Borobia *E* 34 B2
Borox *E* 41 A6
Borriol *E* 44 A3
Bòssost *E* 28 C1
Botão *P* 30 D2
Boticas *P* 30 B3
Botorrita *E* 35 B4
Bóveda *E* 23 C4
Boveda *E* 25 C6
Bràfim *E* 36 C2
Braga *P* 30 B2
Bragança *P* 31 A5
Brañosera *E* 25 C4
Braojos *E* 33 C5
Brazatortas *E* 41 D5
Brea *E* 34 B3
Brea de Tajo *E* 42 A2
Breda *E* 37 B5
Brenes *E* 50 C2
Bretocino *E* 32 A1
Brihuega *E* 33 D6
Brinches *P* 49 B4
Brincones *E* 31 C6
Briones *E* 25 C6
Britelo *P* 30 A2
Briviesca *E* 25 C5
Bronchales *E* 34 D3
Brotas *P* 38 D3
Broto *E* 27 C5
Brozas *E* 39 B6
Brunete *E* 33 D4
Buarcos *P* 38 A2
Bucelas *P* 38 D2
Budens *P* 48 D2
Budia *E* 33 D6
Bueña *E* 35 D4
Buenache de Alarcón *E* 42 B3
Buenache de la Sierra *E* 43 A4
Buenaventura *E* 41 A4

Buenavista de Valdavia *E* 24 C3
Buendía *E* 34 D1
Bueu *E* 22 D2
Bugarra *E* 43 B6
Buitrago del Lozoya *E* 33 C5
Bujalance *E* 51 B5
Bujaraloz *E* 35 B5
Bullas *E* 53 B6
Buniel *E* 25 D5
Buñol *E* 43 C6
Bunyola *E* 46 B3
Burbáguena *E* 34 C3
Burganes de Valverde *E* 32 A1
Burgau *P* 48 D2
Burgohondo *E* 32 D3
Burgos *E* 25 D5
Burgui *E* 27 C4
Burguillos *E* 50 C2
Burguillos del Cerro *E* 49 A6
Burguillos de Toledo *E* 41 B5
Burjassot *E* 44 C2
Burlada *E* 26 C3
Burón *E* 24 B3
Burriana *E* 44 B3
Burujón *E* 41 B5
Busot *E* 55 A4
Bustillo del Páramo *E* 24 D1
Busturi-Axpe *E* 25 B6

C

Cabacés *E* 36 C1
Cabañaquinta *E* 24 B2
Cabañas del Castillo *E* 40 B3
Cabanas de Viriato *P* 30 D3
Cabañas Raras *E* 23 C5
Cabanes *E* 44 A3
Cabanillas *E* 26 D3
Cabeça Gorda *P* 49 B4
Cabeção *P* 39 D4
Cabeceiras de Basto *P* 30 B3
Cabeço de Vide *P* 39 C4
Cabeza de Framontanos *E* 31 C6
Cabeza del Buey *E* 40 D3
Cabeza del Caballo *E* 31 C5
Cabeza la Vaca *E* 50 B1
Cabezamesada *E* 42 B2
Cabezarados *E* 41 D5
Cabezarrubias del Puerto *E* 41 D5
Cabezas del Villar *E* 32 D2
Cabezas Rubias *E* 49 C5
Cabezón de Cameros *E* 26 D1
Cabezón de la Sal *E* 25 B4
Cabezón de Liébana *E* 24 B3
Cabezuela del Valle *E* 40 A2
Cabo de Palos *E* 54 C3
Cabolafuente *E* 34 C2
Cabra *E* 51 C5
Cabração *P* 30 A2

Cabra del Camp *E* 36 B2
Cabra del Santo Cristo *E* 52 C3
Cabra de Mora *E* 43 A6
Cabrejas del Pinar *E* 33 A6
Cabrela *P* 38 D3
Cabril *P* 39 A4
Cabrillanes *E* 23 C6
Cabrillas *E* 31 D6
Cacabelos *E* 23 C5
Caçarelhos *P* 31 B6
Cacém *P* 38 D1
Cáceres *E* 40 C1
Cachopo *P* 49 D4
Cacín *E* 51 D6
Cadalso de los Vidrios *E* 41 A5
Cadaqués *E* 29 D6
Cadaval *P* 38 C2
Cádiar *E* 52 D3
Cádiz *E* 56 B2
Cadreita *E* 26 D3
Cadrete *E* 35 B4
Caión *E* 22 B2
Cala *E* 50 B2
Calabardina *E* 53 C6
Calaceite *E* 35 C6
Cala d'Or *E* 47 C4
Cala en Porter *E* 47 B6
Calaf *E* 36 B3
Calafell *E* 36 C3
Cala Figuera *E* 47 C4
Calahonda *E* 58 B3
Calahorra *E* 26 D2
Cala Millor *E* 47 B5
Calamocha *E* 34 C3
Calamonte *E* 40 D1
Cala Murada *E* 47 C4
Calañas *E* 49 C6
Calanda *E* 35 C5
Cala Rajada *E* 47 B5
Cala Santa Galdana *E* 47 B6
Calasparra *E* 53 B6
Calatayud *E* 34 B3
Calatorao *E* 34 B3
Caldas da Rainha *P* 38 C2
Caldas de Mombuy *E* 37 B4
Caldas de Reis *E* 22 C2
Caldas de Vizela *P* 30 B2
Caldearenas *E* 27 D5
Caldelas *P* 30 B2
Caldelas Taipas *P* 30 B2
Caldes de Malavella *E* 37 A5
Caldes de Montbui *E* 37 B4
Caldes d'Estrac *E* 37 B4
Calella *E* 37 B5
Calendário *P* 30 B2
Calera de León *E* 50 B2
Calera y Chozas *E* 41 B4
Caleruega *E* 33 A5
Cálig *E* 35 D6
Callosa d'En Sarrià *E* 44 D3
Callosa de Segura *E* 54 B3
Calomarde *E* 34 D3
Calonge *E* 37 A5

Calp *E* 44 D3
Calpe *E* 44 D3
Caltojar *E* 33 B6
Calvão *P* 30 D2
Calvarrasa de Abajo *E* 32 C2
Calvarrasa de Arriba *E* 32 C2
Calvos *E* 30 A3
Calzada de Calatrava *E* 41 D6
Calzada de Valdunciel *E* 32 C1
Calzadilla *E* 39 A6
Calzadilla de los Barros *E* 50 A2
Camaleño *E* 24 B3
Camallera *E* 29 D5
Camañas *E* 35 D4
Camarasa *E* 36 A2
Camarena *E* 41 A5
Camarena de la Sierra *E* 43 A5
Camarillas *E* 35 D4
Camariñas *E* 22 B1
Camarzana de Tera *E* 31 A6
Camas *E* 50 C2
Cambados *E* 22 D2
Cambil *E* 52 C2
Cambra de Baixo *P* 30 D3
Cambre *E* 22 B2
Cambrils *E* 36 C2
Camerles *E* 36 D1
Caminha *P* 30 A2
Caminomorisco *E* 31 D6
Caminreal *E* 34 C3
Campanario *E* 40 D3
Campanet *E* 47 B4
Campano *E* 56 C3
Campaspero *E* 33 B4
Campdevànol *E* 29 D4
Campeã *P* 30 B3
Campello *E* 55 A4
Campelo *E* 38 A3
Campelos *P* 38 C2
Campillo de Alto Buey *E* 43 B4
Campillo de Arenas *E* 51 C6
Campillo de Dueñas *E* 34 C3
Campillo de Llerena *E* 50 A2
Campillos *E* 51 D4
Campillos-Paravientos *E* 43 B5
Campinho *E* 49 A5
Campisábalos *E* 33 C6
Campo *E* 27 D6
Campo *P* 30 B2
Campo de Caso *E* 24 B2
Campo de Criptana *E* 42 C2
Campo de San Pedro *E* 33 B5
Campofrío *E* 49 C6
Campo Lugar *E* 40 C2
Campo Maior *P* 39 D5
Camponaraya *E* 23 C5
Campo Redondo *P* 48 C3
Camporrells *E* 36 A1

Camporrobles *E* **43** B5
Campos *P* **30** B3
Campos del Puerto *E* **47** C4
Campotéjar *E* **51** C6
Camprodon *E* **29** D4
Camuñas *E* **41** C6
Cañada *E* **43** D6
Cañada de Benatanduz *E* **35** D5
Cañada del Hoyo *E* **43** B4
Cañada Vellida *E* **35** D4
Canalejas del Arroyo *E* **34** D1
Canalejas de Peñafiel *E* **33** B4
Canals *E* **43** D6
Cañamares *E* **34** D2
Cañamero *E* **40** C3
Cañaveral *E* **40** B1
Cañaveral de León *E* **49** B6
Cañaveras *E* **34** D2
Cañaveruelas *E* **34** D1
Cancarix *E* **53** A6
Candanchú *E* **27** C5
Candás *E* **24** A1
Candasnos *E* **35** B6
Candelario *E* **32** D1
Candeleda *E* **40** A3
Candemil *P* **30** A2
Candilichera *E* **34** B2
Candín *E* **23** C5
Canedo *P* **30** C2
Canena *E* **52** B3
Canero *E* **23** A6
Canet de Mar *E* **37** B5
Cañete *E* **43** A4
Cañete de las Torres *E* **51** B5
Cañete la Real *E* **51** D4
Canet lo Roig *E* **35** D6
Cangas *E* **22** D2
Cangas del Narcea *E* **23** B5
Cangas de Onís *E* **24** B2
Canha *P* **38** D3
Canhestros *P* **48** B3
Canicosa de la Sierra *E* **33** A6
Caniles *E* **53** C4
Canillas de Aceituno *E* **51** D6
Cañizal *E* **32** C2
Cañizares *E* **34** D2
Cañizo *E* **32** A2
Canjáyar *E* **53** D4
Cano *P* **39** D4
Cánovas *E* **54** C2
Can Pastilla *E* **46** B3
Can Picafort *E* **47** B4
Canredondo *E* **34** C1
Cantalapiedra *E* **32** C2
Cantalejo *E* **33** C4
Cantalpino *E* **32** C2
Cantanhede *P* **30** D2
Cantavieja *E* **35** D5
Canteras *E* **54** C3
Cantillana *E* **50** C2
Cantimpalos *E* **33** C4

Cantoria *E* **53** D5
Canyelles *E* **36** B3
Capafonts *E* **36** B2
Caparica *P* **38** D2
Caparrosa *P* **30** D3
Caparroso *E* **26** D3
Cap-Blanc *E* **44** C3
Capdepera *E* **47** B5
Capileira *E* **52** D3
Capilla *E* **40** D3
Capinha *P* **39** A5
Carabaña *E* **42** A2
Caracuel de Calatrava *E* **41** D5
Caramulo *P* **30** D3
Caranga *E* **23** B6
Caranguejeira *P* **38** B2
Carapinheira *P* **38** A3
Caravaca de la Cruz *E* **53** B6
Carbajales de Alba *E* **31** B6
Carballeda de Avia *E* **22** D3
Carballo *E* **22** B2
Carballo *E* **22** D3
Carbellino *E* **31** C6
Carbonera de Frentes *E* **34** A1
Carboneras *E* **53** D6
Carboneras de Guadazaón *E* **43** B4
Carbonero El Mayor *E* **33** C4
Carboneros *E* **51** B6
Carcaboso *E* **40** A2
Carcabuey *E* **51** C5
Carcaixent *E* **44** C2
Carção *P* **31** B5
Cárcar *E* **26** D2
Carcastillo *E* **26** D3
Carcelén *E* **43** C5
Carchelejo *E* **51** C6
Cardedeu *E* **37** B4
Cardeña *E* **51** B5
Cardeñadijo *E* **25** D5
Cardenete *E* **43** B4
Cardeñosa *E* **32** D3
Cardigos *P* **39** B4
Cardona *E* **36** A3
Cardosas *P* **48** D3
Carenas *E* **34** B3
Caria *P* **39** A5
Caridade *P* **49** A5
Cariñena *E* **35** B4
Cariño *E* **22** A3
Carlet *E* **43** C6
Carmena *E* **41** B5
Cármenes *E* **24** C2
Carmona *E* **50** C3
Carmonita *E* **40** C1
Carnota *E* **22** C1
Carpio *E* **32** C2
Carracedelo *E* **23** C5
Carral *E* **22** B2
Carranque *E* **41** A6
Carrapateira *P* **48** D2
Carrapichana *P* **31** D4
Carrascal del Obispo *E* **31** C6

Carrascosa *E* **34** D2
Carrascosa del Campo *E* **42** A2
Carratraca *E* **57** B5
Carrazeda de Ansiães *P* **31** C4
Carrazedo de Montenegro *P* **31** B4
Carreço *P* **30** A1
Carregado *P* **38** D2
Carregal do Sal *P* **30** D3
Carregueiros *P* **38** B3
Carreira *P* **38** B2
Carreña *E* **24** B3
Carreteira *E* **22** C3
Carriazo *E* **25** B5
Carriço *P* **38** B2
Carrio *E* **22** B3
Carrión de Calatrava *E* **41** D6
Carrión de los Céspedes *E* **50** C2
Carrión de los Condes *E* **24** D3
Carrizo de la Ribera *E* **24** C1
Carrizosa *E* **42** D2
Cartagena *E* **54** C3
Cártama *E* **57** B5
Cartaxo *E* **38** C2
Cartaya *E* **49** D5
Cartes *E* **25** B4
Carucedo *E* **23** D5
Carvalhal *P* **38** B3
Carvalhal *P* **48** A2
Carvalho de Egas *P* **31** B4
Carvalhosa *P* **30** B2
Carviçais *P* **31** C5
Carvoeira *P* **38** C2
Carvoeiro *P* **48** D3
Casabermeja *E* **51** D5
Casa Branca *P* **39** D4
Casa Branca *P* **48** A3
Casalarreina *E* **25** C6
Casarabonela *E* **57** B5
Casar de Cáceres *E* **40** B1
Casar de Palomero *E* **31** D6
Casarejos *E* **33** A6
Casares *E* **23** B6
Casares *E* **57** B4
Casares de las Hurdes *E* **31** D6
Casariche *E* **51** D4
Casarrubios del Monte *E* **41** A5
Casas Altas *E* **43** A5
Casas Bajas *E* **43** A5
Casas de Benitez *E* **43** C4
Casas de Don Pedro *E* **40** C3
Casas de Fernando Alonso *E* **42** C3
Casas de Haro *E* **42** C3
Casas de Juan Gil *E* **43** C5
Casas de Juan Núñez *E* **43** C5

Casas de Lázaro *E* **42** D3
Casas del Monte *E* **40** A2
Casas de los Pinos *E* **42** C3
Casas del Puerto *E* **54** A2
Casas de Millán *E* **40** B1
Casas de Reina *E* **50** B2
Casas de Ves *E* **43** C5
Casas-Ibáñez *E* **43** C5
Casasimarro *E* **43** C4
Casas Novas de Mares *P* **49** A5
Casasola de Arión *E* **32** B2
Casatejada *E* **40** B2
Casavieja *E* **41** A4
Cascais *P* **38** D1
Cascante *E* **26** D3
Cascante del Río *E* **43** A5
Casebres *P* **48** A3
Cáseda *E* **26** C3
Caseras *E* **35** C6
Casével *P* **48** C3
Casillas *E* **32** D3
Casillas de Flores *E* **31** D5
Casinos *E* **43** B6
Caspe *E* **35** C6
Cassà de la Selva *E* **37** A5
Casserres *E* **28** D3
Castalla *E* **54** A3
Castañar de Ibor *E* **40** B3
Castañares de Rioja *E* **25** C6
Castanheira *P* **31** C4
Castanheira de Pêra *P* **38** A3
Castejón *E* **26** D3
Castejón del Puente *E* **35** A6
Castejón de Monegros *E* **35** B5
Castejón de Sos *E* **27** C6
Castejón de Valdejasa *E* **35** A4
Castel de Cabra *E* **35** D5
Casteleiro *P* **39** A5
Castelflorite *E* **35** A6
Castellanos de Castro *E* **25** D4
Castellar de la Frontera *E* **57** C4
Castellar de la Muela *E* **34** C3
Castellar de la Ribera *E* **28** D3
Castellar de Santiago *E* **52** A3
Castellar de Santisteban *E* **52** B3
Castelldans *E* **36** B1
Castell de Cabres *E* **35** D6
Castell de Castells *E* **44** D3
Castelldefels *E* **37** B4
Castell de Ferro *E* **58** B3
Castellfort *E* **35** D5
Castellnou de Bassella *E* **28** D2
Castellnovo *E* **43** B6
Castelló de Farfanya *E* **36** A1
Castelló de la Plana *E* **44** B3

Castelló d'Empúries *E* 29 D5
Castelló de Rugat *E* 44 D2
Castellote *E* 35 D5
Castellserá *E* 36 A2
Castellterçol *E* 37 B4
Castelo Bom *P* 31 D5
Castelo Branco *P* 31 B5
Castelo Branco *P* 39 B5
Castelo de Paiva *P* 30 C2
Castelo de Vide *P* 39 C5
Castelo do Neiva *P* 30 B2
Castelões *P* 30 C3
Castelseras *E* 35 C5
Castielfabib *E* 43 A5
Castiello de Jaca *E* 27 C5
Castilblanco *E* 40 C3
Castilblanco de los Arroyos *E* 50 C2
Castiliscar *E* 27 D4
Castilleja de la Cuesta *E* 50 C2
Castillejar *E* 53 C4
Castillejo de Martin Viejo *E* 31 D5
Castillejo de Mesleón *E* 33 B5
Castillejo de Robledo *E* 33 B5
Castillo de Bayuela *E* 41 A4
Castillo de Garcimuñoz *E* 42 B3
Castillo de Locubín *E* 51 C6
Castillo-Nuevo *E* 27 C4
Castilruiz *E* 34 A2
Castrejón de la Peña *E* 24 C3
Castrelo do Val *E* 31 A4
Castril *E* 53 C4
Castrillo de Don Juan *E* 33 A4
Castrillo de Duero *E* 33 B4
Castrillo de la Reina *E* 33 A6
Castrillo de la Vega *E* 33 B5
Castrillo Tejeriego *E* 33 B4
Castro *E* 23 D4
Castrobarto *E* 25 B5
Castrocalbón *E* 23 D6
Castro Caldelas *E* 23 D4
Castrocontrigo *E* 23 D6
Castro Daire *P* 30 C3
Castro del Río *E* 51 C5
Castro de Ouro *E* 23 A4
Castro de Rei *E* 23 B4
Castrogonzalo *E* 32 A2
Castrojeriz *E* 25 D4
Castro Laboreiro *P* 30 A3
Castro Marim *P* 49 D5
Castromocho *E* 24 D3
Castromonte *E* 32 A3
Castronuevo *E* 32 B2
Castronuño *E* 32 B2
Castropodame *E* 23 C6
Castropol *E* 23 A5
Castro-Urdiales *E* 25 B6
Castroverde *E* 23 B4
Castro Verde *P* 49 C4

Castroverde de Campos *E* 32 A2
Castuera *E* 40 D3
Catadau *E* 43 C6
Catarroja *E* 44 C2
Catí *E* 35 D6
Cativelos *P* 30 D3
Catoira *E* 22 C2
Catral *E* 54 B3
Caudete *E* 43 D6
Caudete de las Fuentes *E* 43 B5
Caudiel *E* 43 B6
Cavaleiro *P* 48 C2
Caxarias *P* 38 B3
Cazalegas *E* 41 A4
Cazalilla *E* 51 B6
Cazalla de la Sierra *E* 50 B3
Cazorla *E* 53 B4
Cea *E* 22 D3
Cea *E* 24 D3
Ceanuri-Elexondo *E* 25 B6
Cebolla *E* 41 B4
Cebreros *E* 33 D4
Ceclavín *E* 39 B6
Cedães *P* 31 B4
Cedeira *E* 22 A3
Cedillo *E* 39 B5
Cedillo del Condado *E* 41 A5
Cedrillas *E* 35 D4
Cee *E* 22 C1
Cehegín *E* 53 B6
Ceinos de Campos *E* 24 D2
Ceira *P* 38 A3
Celadas *E* 35 D4
Celanova *E* 22 D3
Celeiros *P* 30 B2
Cella *E* 35 D4
Celorico da Beira *P* 31 D4
Celorico de Basto *P* 30 B3
Celrà *E* 29 D5
Cenicero *E* 26 C1
Cenicientos *E* 41 A5
Centelles *E* 37 A4
Cercal *P* 38 C2
Cercal *P* 48 C3
Cercedilla *E* 33 D4
Cerdanyola del Vallès *E* 37 B4
Cerdedo *E* 22 D2
Cerdeira *P* 39 A4
Cerezo de Abajo *E* 33 C5
Cerezo de Arriba *E* 33 C5
Cerezo de Ríotirón *E* 25 C6
Cernache do Bonjardim *P* 38 B3
Cernégula *E* 25 C5
Cerralbo *E* 31 C5
Cerva *P* 30 B3
Cervatos de la Cueza *E* 24 D3
Cervera *E* 36 B2
Cervera de la Cañada *E* 34 B3

Cervera del Llano *E* 42 B3
Cervera del Maestre *E* 35 D6
Cervera de los Montes *E* 41 A4
Cervera del Río Alhama *E* 26 D2
Cervera de Pisuerga *E* 24 C3
Cervo *E* 23 A4
Cespedosa *E* 32 D2
Cesuras *E* 22 B3
Cetina *E* 34 B2
Ceutí *E* 54 B2
Cevico de la Torre *E* 33 A4
Cevico Navero *E* 33 A4
Chã *P* 30 A3
Chacim *P* 31 B5
Chalamera *E* 35 B6
Chamusca *P* 38 C3
Chança *P* 39 C4
Chancelaria *P* 38 B3
Chañe *E* 33 B4
Chantada *E* 22 C3
Chao *E* 22 B3
Chapinería *E* 33 D4
Chauchina *E* 51 D6
Chaves *P* 31 A4
Checa *E* 34 D3
Cheles *E* 49 A5
Chella *E* 43 D6
Chelva *E* 43 B6
Chera *E* 43 B6
Chert *E* 35 D6
Cheste *E* 43 C6
Chiclana de la Frontera *E* 56 B3
Chiclana de Segura *E* 52 B3
Chilches *E* 44 B3
Chillón *E* 41 D4
Chilluévar *E* 52 B3
Chiloeches *E* 33 D6
Chimeneas *E* 51 D6
Chinchilla de Monte Aragón *E* 43 D4
Chinchón *E* 41 A6
Chipiona *E* 56 B2
Chiprana *E* 35 C5
Chirivel *E* 53 C5
Chiva *E* 43 C6
Chouto *P* 38 C3
Chovar *E* 44 B2
Chozas de Abajo *E* 24 C1
Chulilla *E* 43 B6
Ciborro *P* 38 D3
Cidones *E* 34 A1
Ciempozuelos *E* 41 A6
Cieza *E* 53 B6
Cifuentes *E* 34 D1
Cigales *E* 32 A3
Cillas *E* 34 C3
Cilleros *E* 39 A6
Cimanes del Tejar *E* 24 C1
Cimballa *E* 34 C3
Cinco Casas *E* 42 C2
Cinctorres *E* 35 D5
Ciñera *E* 24 C2

Cinfães *P* 30 C3
Cintruénigo *E* 26 D3
Cirat *E* 43 A6
Cirauqui *E* 26 C2
Ciria *E* 34 B2
Ciruelos *E* 41 B6
Ciruelos del Pinar *E* 34 C2
Cisneros *E* 24 D3
Cistierna *E* 24 C2
Ciudad Real *E* 41 D6
Ciudad Rodrigo *E* 31 D5
Ciutadella de Menorca *E* 47 B5
Coaña *E* 23 A5
Cobeja *E* 41 A6
Cobeta *E* 34 C2
Coca *E* 32 C3
Cocentaina *E* 44 D2
Codos *E* 34 B3
Cofrentes *E* 43 C5
Cogeces del Monte *E* 33 B4
Cogollos *E* 25 D5
Cogollos Vega *E* 52 D2
Cogolludo *E* 33 C6
Cogula *P* 31 C4
Coimbra *P* 38 A3
Coimbrão *P* 38 B2
Coín *E* 57 B5
Coja *P* 39 A4
Colares *P* 38 D1
Colindres *E* 25 B5
Collado Hermoso *E* 33 C4
Collado Villalba *E* 33 D4
Collanzo *E* 24 B2
Colmeal *P* 39 A4
Colmenar *E* 51 D5
Colmenar del Arroyo *E* 33 D4
Colmenar de Montemayor *E* 31 D6
Colmenar de Oreja *E* 41 A6
Colmenar Viejo *E* 33 D5
Colombres *E* 24 B3
Colomers *E* 29 D5
Colònia de Sant Jordi *E* 47 C4
Colònia de Sant Pere *E* 47 B4
Colos *E* 48 C3
Colunga *E* 24 A2
Comares *E* 57 B6
Comillas *E* 25 B4
Cómpeta *E* 58 B2
Comporta *P* 48 A2
Conceição *P* 49 D4
Concha *E* 25 B5
Condeixa-a-Nova *P* 38 A3
Congosto *E* 23 C5
Congosto de Valdavia *E* 24 C3
Conil de la Frontera *E* 56 C3
Conquista *E* 51 A5
Consell *E* 47 B4
Constância *P* 38 C3
Constantí *E* 36 C2

Constantim *P* 30 B3
Constantim *P* 31 B6
Constantina *E* 50 B3
Constanzana *E* 32 C3
Consuegra *E* 41 C6
Copons *E* 36 B3
Corbalán *E* 35 D4
Corbera *E* 44 C2
Corbera d'Ebre *E* 36 C1
Corçà *E* 37 A5
Corcubión *E* 22 C1
Córdoba *E* 51 B4
Cordobilla de Lácara *E* 40 C1
Corduente *E* 34 C2
Corella *E* 26 D3
Coreses *E* 32 B2
Coria *E* 39 A6
Coria del Río *E* 50 D2
Coripe *E* 50 D3
Corme Porto *E* 22 B1
Cornago *E* 26 D2
Cornellà de Llobregat *E* 37 B4
Cornellà de Terri *E* 29 D5
Cornellana *E* 23 B6
Cornudella de Montsant *E* 36 C2
Cornudilla *E* 25 C5
Corral de Almaguer *E* 42 B2
Corral de Calatrava *E* 41 D5
Corrales *E* 32 B1
Corral-Rubio *E* 43 D5
Corteconcepción *E* 50 B1
Corte de Peleas *E* 39 D6
Cortegada *E* 22 D3
Cortegana *E* 49 B6
Cortes *E* 34 A3
Cortes de Aragón *E* 35 C4
Cortes de Arenoso *E* 43 A6
Cortes de Baza *E* 53 C4
Cortes de la Frontera *E* 57 B4
Cortes de Pallás *E* 43 C6
Cortiçadas do Lavre *P* 38 D3
Cortijo de Arriba *E* 41 C5
Cortijos Nuevos *E* 53 B4
Coruche *P* 38 D3
Corullón *E* 23 C5
Corvera *E* 54 C3
Cosa *E* 35 C4
Coscurita *E* 34 B1
Coslada *E* 33 D5
Costa da Caparica *P* 38 D2
Cosuenda *E* 34 B3
Couço *P* 38 D3
Coura *P* 30 A2
Couto de Cima *P* 30 D3
Covaleda *E* 33 A6
Covarrubias *E* 25 D5
Covilhã *P* 39 A5
Cox *E* 54 B3
Cózar *E* 42 D2
Crato *P* 39 C4
Crecente *E* 22 D3

Crémenes *E* 24 C2
Crespos *E* 32 C3
Cretas *E* 35 C6
Crevillente *E* 54 B3
Cripán *E* 26 C1
Cristóbal *E* 32 D1
Cuacos de Yuste *E* 40 A2
Cuadros *E* 24 C2
Cualedro *E* 31 A4
Cuarte de Huerva *E* 35 B4
Cuba *P* 49 B4
Cubalhão *P* 30 A3
Cubells *E* 36 A2
Cubla *E* 43 A5
Cubo de Bureba *E* 25 C6
Cubo de la Solana *E* 34 B2
Cucalón *E* 35 C4
Cudillero *E* 23 A6
Cuéllar *E* 33 B4
Cuenca *E* 43 A4
Cuenca de Campos *E* 24 D3
Cuerva *E* 41 B5
Cueva de Agreda *E* 34 A3
Cuevas Bajas *E* 51 D5
Cuevas de Almanzora *E* 53 D6
Cuevas del Becerro *E* 57 A5
Cuevas del Campo *E* 53 C4
Cuevas de San Clemente *E* 25 D5
Cuevas de San Marcos *E* 51 D5
Cuevas de Vinromá *E* 44 A3
Cuevas Labradas *E* 35 D4
Culla *E* 35 D5
Cúllar-Baza *E* 53 C4
Cullera *E* 44 C3
Cumbres de San Bartolomé *E* 49 B6
Cumbres Mayores *E* 49 B6
Cumeada *P* 48 D3
Cumieira *P* 30 B3
Cunha *P* 31 C4
Cunit *E* 36 C3
Cuntis *E* 22 C2
Currás *E* 22 C2

D

Daganzo de Arriba *E* 33 D5
Daimiel *E* 41 C6
Dalías *E* 59 B4
Daroca *E* 34 C3
Darque *P* 30 B2
Darro *E* 52 D3
Deba *E* 26 B2
Degaña *E* 23 C5
Dehesa de Campoamor *E* 54 B3
Dehesas de Guadix *E* 52 C3
Deià *E* 46 B3
Deifontes *E* 51 D6
Deilão *P* 31 A5
Deleitosa *E* 40 B2

Deltebre *E* 36 D1
Denia *E* 44 D3
Descargamaría *E* 31 D6
Destriana *E* 23 D6
Deza *E* 34 B2
Diego Álvaro *E* 32 D2
Diezma *E* 52 D3
Dilar *E* 51 D6
Dobro *E* 25 C5
Dolores *E* 54 B3
Domingo Pérez *E* 41 B4
Don Álvaro *E* 40 D1
Doña Mencía *E* 51 C5
Don Benito *E* 40 D2
Done Bikendi Harana *E* 26 C2
Doneztebe *E* 26 B3
Doñinos de Salamanca *E* 32 C1
Donostia - San Sebastián *E* 26 B2
Dornelas *P* 30 B3
Dos Aguas *E* 43 C6
Dosbarrios *E* 41 B6
Dos Hermanas *E* 50 D2
Dos Torres *E* 51 A4
Driebes *E* 42 A2
Duas Igrejas *P* 31 B6
Dueñas *E* 32 A3
Dumbría *E* 22 C1
Durana *E* 26 C1
Durango *E* 26 B1
Dúrcal *E* 52 D2
Duruelo de la Sierra *E* 33 A6

E

Echarri *E* 26 C3
Écija *E* 51 C4
Edrosa *P* 31 A5
Edroso *P* 31 B5
Eibar *E* 26 B2
Eivissa *E* 45 D6
Eja *P* 30 C2
Ejea de los Caballeros *E* 27 D4
Ejulve *E* 35 D5
El Álamo *E* 41 A5
El Algar *E* 54 C3
El Almendro *E* 49 C5
El Alquián *E* 59 B5
El Arahal *E* 50 D3
El Arenal *E* 40 A3
El Astillero *E* 25 B5
El Ballestero *E* 42 D3
El Barco de Ávila *E* 32 D2
El Barco de Valdeorras *E* 23 D5
El Barraco *E* 32 D3
El Bodón *E* 31 D5
El Bonillo *E* 42 D3
El Bosque *E* 57 B4
El Bullaque *E* 41 C5
El Burgo *E* 57 B5

El Burgo de Ebro *E* 35 B4
El Burgo de Osma *E* 33 B6
El Burgo Ranero *E* 24 D2
El Buste *E* 34 A3
El Cabaco *E* 31 D6
El Cabildo y la Campana *E* 53 C6
El Cabo de Gata *E* 59 B5
El Campillo *E* 49 C6
El Campillo de la Jara *E* 40 B3
El Campo de Peñaranda *E* 32 C2
El Cañavate *E* 42 C3
El Carpio *E* 51 B5
El Carpio de Tajo *E* 41 B5
El Casar *E* 33 D5
El Casar de Escalona *E* 41 A4
El Castellar *E* 35 D4
El Castillo de las Guardas *E* 50 C2
El Catllar de Gaià *E* 36 C2
El Centenillo *E* 51 A6
El Cerro de Andévalo *E* 49 C6
Elche de la Sierra *E* 53 A5
Elche-Elx *E* 54 B3
Elciego *E* 26 C1
El Coronil *E* 50 D3
El Cubo de Don Sancho *E* 31 C6
El Cubo de Tierra del Vino *E* 32 C1
El Cuervo *E* 43 A5
El Cuervo *E* 56 B3
Elda *E* 54 A3
El Ejido *E* 59 B4
El Escorial *E* 33 D4
El Espinar *E* 33 D4
El Estrecho *E* 54 C3
El Fresno *E* 32 D3
El Garrobo *E* 50 C2
Elgeta *E* 26 B2
Elgoibar *E* 26 B2
El Grado *E* 27 D6
El Granado *E* 49 C5
El Grau de Borriana *E* 44 B3
El Herrumblar *E* 43 C4
El Hito *E* 42 B3
El Hoyo de Pinares *E* 33 D4
Elizalde *E* 26 B3
Elizondo *E* 26 B3
Eljas *E* 39 A6
El Llano *E* 23 B4
El Losar del Barco *E* 32 D2
El Masroig *E* 36 C1
El Molar *E* 33 D5
El Molinillo *E* 41 C5
El Moral *E* 53 B5
El Morell *E* 36 C2
Elorrio *E* 26 B1
Elorz *E* 26 C3
El Oso *E* 32 C3
El Palmar *E* 54 B3

El Palo *E* **57** B6
El Payo *E* **39** A6
El Pedernoso *E* **42** C2
El Pedroso *E* **50** B3
El Pedroso de la Armuña *E* **32** C2
El Peral *E* **43** C4
El Perdigón *E* **32** B1
El Perelló *E* **36** C1
El Perelló *E* **44** C2
El Picazo *E* **43** C4
El Pinell de Bray *E* **36** C1
El Piñero *E* **32** B2
El Pla de Santa Maria *E* **36** B2
El Pobo *E* **35** D4
El Pobo de Dueñas *E* **34** D3
El Pont d'Armentera *E* **36** B2
El Port *E* **44** B3
El Port de la Selva *E* **29** D6
El Prat de Llobregat *E* **37** B4
El Provencio *E* **42** C3
El Puente *E* **25** B5
El Puente de Arzobispo *E* **40** B3
El Puerto de Santa María *E* **56** B2
El Real de la Jara *E* **50** B2
El Real de San Vicente *E* **41** A4
El Recuenco *E* **34** D2
El Robledo *E* **41** C5
El Rocío *E* **50** D1
El Romeral *E* **41** B6
El Rompido *E* **49** D5
El Ronquillo *E* **50** C2
El Royo *E* **34** A1
El Rubio *E* **51** C4
El Sabinar *E* **27** D4
El Sabinar *E* **53** B5
El Saler *E* **44** C2
El Salobral *E* **43** D4
Els Arcs *E* **36** B2
El Saucejo *E* **51** D4
El Saugo *E* **31** D5
El Serrat *AND* **28** C3
El Soleràs *E* **36** B1
Els Prats de Rei *E* **36** B3
El Tiemblo *E* **32** D3
El Toboso *E* **42** C2
El Torno *E* **40** A2
El Trincheto *E* **41** C5
El Tumbalejo *E* **49** C6
Elvas *P* **39** D5
El Vendrell *E* **36** C3
El Verger *E* **44** D3
El Villar de Arnedo *E* **26** D2
El Viso *E* **51** A4
El Viso del Alcor *E* **50** C3
Embid *E* **34** C3
Embid de Ariza *E* **34** B2
Encamp *AND* **28** C3
Encinas de Abajo *E* **32** C2
Encinasola *E* **49** B6
Encinas Reales *E* **51** D5
Encinedo *E* **23** D5

Enciso *E* **26** D2
Endrinal *E* **32** D1
Enfesta *E* **22** C2
Enguera *E* **43** D6
Enguidanos *E* **43** B4
Enix *E* **59** B4
Entradas *P* **49** C4
Entrena *E* **26** D1
Entroncamento *P* **38** C3
Envendos *P* **39** B4
Épila *E* **35** B4
Erandio *E* **25** B6
Erice *E* **26** C3
Ericeira *P* **38** D1
Erla *E* **27** D4
Ermelo *P* **30** B3
Ermesinde *P* **30** C2
Ermidas do Sado *P* **48** B3
Ermua *E* **26** B2
Errenteria *E* **26** B2
Errezil *E* **26** B2
Ervedosa do Douro *P* **31** C4
Ervidel *P* **49** B4
Escairón *E* **23** C4
Escalante *E* **25** B5
Escalhão *P* **31** C5
Escaló *E* **28** C2
Es Caló *E* **45** D6
Escalona *E* **41** A5
Escalona del Prado *E* **33** C4
Escalonilla *E* **41** B5
Escalos de Baixo *P* **39** B5
Escalos de Cima *P* **39** B5
Escamilla *E* **34** D1
Es Canar *E* **45** D6
Escañuela *E* **51** B6
Escariche *E* **33** D6
Escarigo *P* **39** A5
Escároz *E* **27** C4
Escatrón *E* **35** B5
Escombreras *E* **54** C3
Escorca *E* **47** B4
Escorihuela *E* **35** D4
Escucha *E* **35** D4
Escurial *E* **40** C2
Escúzar *E* **51** D6
Esgos *E* **22** D3
Esgueira *P* **30** D2
Esguevillas de Esgueva *E* **33** A4
Eskoriatza *E* **26** B1
Eslava *E* **26** C3
Es Migjorn Gran *E* **47** B6
Espadañedo *E* **23** D6
Esparragalejo *E* **39** D6
Esparragosa *E* **40** D3
Esparragosa de la Serena *E* **40** D3
Esparreguera *E* **36** B3
Esparza de Salazar *E* **27** C4
Espeja *E* **31** D5
Espeja de San Marcelino *E* **33** A6
Espejo *E* **51** C5
Espejón *E* **33** A6

Espera *E* **50** D2
Esperança *P* **39** C5
Espiel *E* **51** B4
Espinama *E* **24** B3
Espinhal *P* **38** A3
Espinho *P* **30** C2
Espinilla *E* **25** B4
Espinosa de Cerrato *E* **33** A4
Espinosa de Henares *E* **33** C6
Espinosa de los Monteros *E* **25** B5
Espinoso del Rey *E* **41** B4
Espírito Santo *P* **49** C4
Espite *P* **38** B3
Esplegares *E* **34** C2
Esplugues de Llobregat *E* **37** B4
Esplús *E* **35** A6
Espolla *E* **29** D5
Esponellà *E* **29** D5
Esporles *E* **46** B3
Esposende *P* **30** B2
Espot *E* **28** C2
Esquivias *E* **41** A6
Estación de Baeza *E* **52** B2
Estadilla *E* **27** D6
Estanyol de Mitjorn *E* **47** C4
Estarreja *P* **30** D2
Este *P* **30** B2
Estela *P* **30** B2
Estella *E* **26** C2
Estellencs *E* **46** B3
Estepa *E* **51** D4
Estepar *E* **25** D4
Estepona *E* **57** B4
Esteras de Medinaceli *E* **34** C2
Estercuel *E* **35** C5
Esterri d'Aneu *E* **28** C2
Estói *P* **49** D4
Estômbar *P* **48** D3
Estoril *P* **38** D1
Estreito *P* **39** B4
Estrela *P* **49** B5
Estremera *E* **42** A2
Estremoz *P* **39** D4
Estriégala *E* **34** C1
Etrín Bajo *E* **39** D6
Etxalar *E* **26** B3
Etxarri-Aranatz *E* **26** C2
Eulate *E* **26** C2
Évora *E* **49** A4
Évora-Monte *P* **39** D4
Extremo *P* **30** A2
Ezcaray *E* **25** D6
Ezkurra *E* **26** B3

F

Fabara *E* **35** C6
Fabero *E* **23** C5
Fábricas de San Juan de Alcaraz *E* **53** A5

Facinas *E* **56** C3
Fafe *P* **30** B3
Failde *P* **31** A5
Fajão *P* **39** A4
Fajarda *P* **38** D3
Falces *E* **26** D3
Falset *E* **36** C2
Famalicão *P* **31** D4
Fanlo *E* **27** C6
Fão *P* **30** B2
Farasdues *E* **27** D4
Fariza de Sayago *E* **31** B6
Farlete *E* **35** B5
Faro *P* **49** D4
Faro do Alentejo *P* **49** B4
Fatela *P* **39** A5
Fátima *P* **38** B3
Faura *E* **44** B2
Favaios *P* **31** B4
Favara *E* **44** C2
Fayón *E* **35** C6
Feijó *P* **38** D2
Feira do Monte *E* **23** B4
Feiteira *P* **49** D4
Felanitx *E* **47** C4
Felgar *P* **31** C5
Felgueiras *P* **30** B3
Félix *E* **59** B4
Fene *E* **22** B3
Férez *E* **53** A5
Feria *E* **49** A6
Fermoselle *E* **31** B6
Fernáncaballero *E* **41** C6
Fernán Núñez *E* **51** C4
Ferreira *E* **23** A4
Ferreira do Alentejo *P* **49** B4
Ferreira do Zêzere *P* **38** B3
Ferrel *P* **38** C1
Ferreras de Abajo *E* **31** A6
Ferreras de Arriba *E* **31** A6
Ferreries *E* **47** B6
Ferreruela de Huerva *E* **35** C4
Ferreruela de Tábara *E* **31** A6
Ferrol *E* **22** B3
Figueira da Foz *P* **38** A2
Figueira de Castelo Rodrigo *P* **31** C5
Figueira e Barros *P* **39** C4
Figueiredo de Alva *P* **30** C3
Figueiró da Granja *P* **31** D4
Figueiró dos Vinhos *P* **38** B3
Figueres *E* **29** D5
Figueroles *E* **44** A3
Figueruela de Arriba *E* **31** A6
Fiñana *E* **53** D4
Finestrat *E* **55** A4
Fiscal *E* **27** C5
Fisterra *E* **22** C1
Fitero *E* **26** D3
Flix *E* **36** C1
Flores de Ávila *E* **32** C2
Florida de Liébana *E* **32** C1
Folgoso de Courel *E* **23** C4
Folgoso de la Ribera *E* **23** C6

Fondevila *E* **30** A3
Fondón *E* **53** D4
Fonelas *E* **52** C3
Fonfría *E* **31** B6
Fonfría *E* **35** C4
Fontanar *E* **33** D6
Fontanarejo *E* **41** C4
Fontanosas *E* **41** D4
Fonte Díaz *E* **22** C2
Fontellas *E* **26** D3
Fontes *P* **38** B3
Fontiveros *E* **32** C3
Fonz *E* **27** D6
Forcall *E* **35** D5
Forcarei *E* **22** C2
Forjães *P* **30** B2
Formiche Alto *E* **43** A6
Fornells *E* **47** A6
Fornells de la Selva *E* **37** A5
Fornos *P* **31** C5
Fornos de Algodres *P* **31** D4
Foros de Vale Figueira *P* **38** D3
Foros do Arrão *P* **38** C3
Fortanete *E* **35** D5
Fortios *P* **39** C5
Fortuna *E* **54** B3
Foz *E* **23** A4
Foz *P* **38** C3
Foz do Arelho *P* **38** C2
Foz Giraldo *P* **39** A4
Frades de la Sierra *E* **32** D1
Fraga *E* **35** B6
Frailes *E* **51** C6
Franco *P* **31** B4
Fratel *P* **39** B4
Frechas *P* **31** B4
Frechilla *E* **24** D3
Fregenal de la Sierra *E* **49** B6
Freginals *E* **36** D1
Freila *E* **53** C4
Freixedas *P* **31** D4
Freixianda *P* **38** B3
Freixiosa *P* **30** D3
Freixo *P* **30** B2
Freixo de Espada à Cinta *P* **31** C5
Fresneda de la Sierra *E* **34** D2
Fresnedoso de Ibor *E* **40** B3
Fresno Alhándiga *E* **32** D2
Fresno de la Ribera *E* **32** B2
Fresno de Sayago *E* **31** B6
Fresno el Viejo *E* **32** C2
Frías *E* **25** C5
Frigiliana *E* **58** B2
Friol *E* **22** B3
Frómista *E* **25** D4
Fronteira *P* **39** C4
Fuencaliente *E* **51** A5
Fuendejalón *E* **34** B3
Fuengirola *E* **57** B5
Fuenlabrada *E* **41** A6
Fuenmayor *E* **26** D1
Fuensalida *E* **41** A5

Fuensanta *E* **43** C4
Fuensanta *E* **53** C6
Fuensanta de Martos *E* **51** C6
Fuente-Álamo *E* **43** D5
Fuente Álamo *E* **54** C3
Fuentealbilla *E* **43** C5
Fuentecambrón *E* **33** B5
Fuentecén *E* **33** B5
Fuente de Cantos *E* **50** B2
Fuente del Arco *E* **50** B2
Fuente del Maestre *E* **50** A1
Fuente de Pedro Naharro *E* **42** B2
Fuente de Piedra *E* **51** D4
Fuente el Fresno *E* **41** C6
Fuente el Saz de Jarama *E* **33** D5
Fuente el Sol *E* **32** C3
Fuenteguinaldo *E* **31** D5
Fuentelapeña *E* **32** B2
Fuentelcésped *E* **33** B5
Fuentelespino de Haro *E* **42** B3
Fuentelespino de Moya *E* **43** B5
Fuentelmonge *E* **34** B2
Fuentenovilla *E* **33** D6
Fuente Obejuna *E* **50** B3
Fuente Palmera *E* **51** C4
Fuentepelayo *E* **33** C4
Fuentepinilla *E* **33** B6
Fuenterodos *E* **35** B4
Fuenterrabía *E* **26** B3
Fuenterrebollo *E* **33** B4
Fuenterroble de Salvatierra *E* **32** D1
Fuentesaúco *E* **32** C2
Fuentesaúco de Fuentidueña *E* **33** B4
Fuentes-Claras *E* **34** C3
Fuentes de Andalucía *E* **50** C3
Fuentes de Ebro *E* **35** B5
Fuentes de Jiloca *E* **34** C3
Fuentes de León *E* **49** B6
Fuentes de Nava *E* **24** D3
Fuentes de Oñoro *E* **31** D5
Fuentes de Ropel *E* **32** A2
Fuentespalda *E* **35** C6
Fuente-Tójar *E* **51** C6
Fuente Vaqueros *E* **51** D6
Fuentidueña *E* **33** B4
Fuerte del Rey *E* **51** B6
Fuertescusa *E* **34** D2
Fundada *P* **38** B3
Fundão *P* **39** A5
Funes *E* **26** D3
Furadouro *P* **30** C2
Fustiñana *E* **26** D3

G

Gabaldón *E* **43** B4

Gabia la Grande *E* **51** D6
Gádor *E* **53** D4
Gaeiras *P* **38** C2
Gafanha da Boa Hora *P* **30** D2
Gafanha da Nazaré *P* **30** D2
Gafanha do Carmo *P* **30** D2
Gafanhoeira *P* **39** D4
Gáfete *P* **39** C4
Gajanejos *E* **33** C6
Galapagar *E* **33** D4
Galaroza *E* **49** B6
Galbarra *E* **26** C2
Galende *E* **23** D5
Galera *E* **53** C4
Galinduste *E* **32** D2
Galisteo *E* **40** B1
Gallegos de Argañán *E* **31** D5
Gallegos de Solmirón *E* **32** D2
Gallur *E* **34** A3
Galve *E* **35** D4
Galve de Sorbe *E* **33** C6
Galveias *P* **39** C4
Gálvez *E* **41** B5
Gama *E* **25** B5
Gandarela *P* **30** B3
Gandesa *E* **35** C6
Gandía *E* **44** D3
Gandra *P* **30** A2
Ganfei *P* **30** A2
Garaballa *E* **43** B5
Garbayuela *E* **41** D4
Garcia *E* **36** C1
Garciaz *E* **40** C2
Garcihernández *E* **32** C2
Garcillán *E* **33** C4
Garcinarro *E* **42** A2
Gargáligas *E* **40** D2
Gargallo *E* **35** C5
Garganta la Olla *E* **40** A2
Garlitos *E* **41** D4
Garrafe de Torio *E* **24** C2
Garralda *E* **26** C3
Garray *E* **34** A2
Garrovillas *E* **39** B6
Garrucha *E* **53** D6
Garvão *P* **48** C3
Gascueña *E* **42** A3
Gata *E* **39** A6
Gata de Gorgos *E* **44** D3
Gátova *E* **43** B6
Gaucín *E* **57** B4
Gavà *E* **37** B4
Gavião *P* **39** C4
Gazolaz *E* **26** C3
Gelsa *E* **35** B5
Génave *E* **53** A4
Genestoso *E* **23** B6
Genevilla *E* **26** C2
Genovés *E* **44** D2
Ger *E* **28** D3
Gerena *E* **50** C2
Gérgal *E* **53** D4

Gerindote *E* **41** B5
Gernika-Lumo *E* **25** B6
Gerona *E* **37** A5
Gestalgar *E* **43** B6
Getafe *E* **41** A6
Getaria *E* **26** B2
Gibraleón *E* **49** C6
Gibraltar *GBZ* **57** C4
Gijón-Xixón *E* **24** A2
Gilena *E* **51** D4
Ginzo de Limia *E* **30** A3
Giões *P* **49** C4
Girona *E* **37** A5
Gironella *E* **28** D3
Glória *P* **39** D4
Glória do Ribatejo *P* **38** C3
Godelleta *E* **43** C6
Góis *P* **39** A4
Goizueta *E* **26** B3
Golegã *P* **38** C3
Golmes *E* **36** B2
Golpejas *E* **31** C6
Gómara *E* **34** B2
Gomecello *E* **32** C2
Gomes Aires *P* **48** C3
Gonçalo *P* **31** D4
Gondomar *E* **22** D2
Gondomar *P* **30** C2
Gopegi *E* **25** C6
Gor *E* **53** D4
Gorafe *E* **52** C3
Gordaliza del Pino *E* **24** D2
Gormaz *E* **33** B6
Gouveia *P* **31** D4
Gove *P* **30** C3
Gradefes *E* **24** C2
Grado *E* **23** B6
Graena *E* **52** D3
Graja de Iniesta *E* **43** C4
Grajal de Campos *E* **24** D3
Granada *E* **52** D2
Granátula de Calatrava *E* **41** D6
Grandas *E* **23** B5
Grândola *P* **48** B3
Grañén *E* **35** A5
Granja *P* **49** A5
Granja de Moreruela *E* **32** A1
Granja de Torrehermosa *E* **50** A3
Granja do Ulmeiro *P* **38** A3
Granollers *E* **37** B4
Gratallops *E* **36** C1
Graus *E* **27** D6
Grávalos *E* **26** D2
Grazalema *E* **57** B4
Grea de Albarracín *E* **34** D3
Griegos *E* **34** D3
Grijota *E* **24** D3
Griñón *E* **41** A6
Grisén *E* **35** B4
Grullos *E* **23** B6
Guadahortuna *E* **52** C3
Guadajoz *E* **50** C3

Guadalajara *E* **33** D6
Guadalaviar *E* **34** D3
Guadalcanal *E* **50** B2
Guadalcázar *E* **51** C4
Guadalest *E* **44** D3
Guadalmez *E* **41** D4
Guadarrama *E* **33** D4
Guadassuar *E* **43** C6
Guadix *E* **52** D3
Guájar-Faraguit *E* **58** B2
Guarda *P* **31** D4
Guardamar del Segura *E* **54** B3
Guardias Viejas *E* **59** B4
Guardiola de Berguedà *E* **28** D3
Guardo *E* **24** C3
Guardramiro *E* **31** C6
Guareña *E* **40** D2
Guaro *E* **57** B5
Guarromán *E* **51** B6
Gudar *E* **35** D4
Guecho *E* **25** B6
Güéjar-Sierra *E* **52** D3
Güeñes *E* **25** B6
Guernica *E* **25** B6
Guerri de la Sal *E* **28** D2
Güesa *E* **27** C4
Guia *P* **38** B2
Guia *P* **48** D3
Guijo de Coria *E* **39** A6
Guijo de Galisteo *E* **40** A1
Guijo de Granadilla *E* **40** A2
Guijuelo *E* **32** D1
Guilhofrei *P* **30** B3
Guilhovai *P* **30** C2
Guillena *E* **50** C2
Guimarães *P* **30** B2
Guisando *E* **40** A3
Guissona *E* **36** A2
Guitiriz *E* **22** B3
Gumiel de Hizán *E* **33** A5
Gumiel de Mercado *E* **33** A5
Gurrea de Gállego *E* **27** D4

H

Hacinas *E* **33** A6
Haro *E* **25** C6
Hecho *E* **27** C4
Helechal *E* **40** D3
Hellín *E* **53** A6
Henarejos *E* **43** B5
Herbés *E* **35** D6
Herencia *E* **42** C1
Herguijuela *E* **40** C2
Hermisende *E* **31** A5
Hernani *E* **26** B2
Hernansancho *E* **32** C3
Herramélluri *E* **25** C6
Herrera *E* **51** C4
Herrera del Duque *E* **41** C4
Herrera de los Navarros *E* **35** C4

Herrera de Pisuerga *E* **25** C4
Herrería *E* **34** C2
Herreruela *E* **39** C6
Hiendelaencina *E* **33** C6
Higuera de Arjona *E* **51** B6
Higuera de la Serena *E* **40** D2
Higuera de la Sierra *E* **50** B1
Higuera de Llerena *E* **50** A2
Higuera de Vargas *E* **49** A6
Higuera la Real *E* **49** B6
Higueruela *E* **43** D5
Higueruelas *E* **43** B6
Híjar *E* **35** C5
Hinojal *E* **40** B1
Hinojales *E* **49** B6
Hinojares *E* **53** C4
Hinojasas de Calatrava *E* **41** D5
Hinojos *E* **50** D1
Hinojosa *E* **34** C2
Hinojosa de Duero *E* **31** C5
Hinojosa de Jarque *E* **35** D4
Hinojosa del Duque *E* **51** A4
Hinojosa del Valle *E* **50** A2
Hinojosa de San Vicente *E* **41** A4
Hita *E* **33** C6
Holguera *E* **40** B1
Hondarribia *E* **26** B3
Hondón de las Nieves *E* **54** B3
Hondón de los Frailes *E* **54** B3
Honrubia *E* **42** B3
Honrubia de la Cuesta *E* **33** B5
Hontacillas *E* **42** B3
Hontalbilla *E* **33** B4
Hontanaya *E* **42** B2
Hontoria de la Cantera *E* **25** D5
Hontoria del Pinar *E* **33** A6
Hontoria de Valdearados *E* **33** A5
Horcajo de las Torres *E* **32** C2
Horcajo de los Montes *E* **41** C4
Horcajo de Santiago *E* **42** B2
Horcajo Medianero *E* **32** D2
Hormilla *E* **25** D6
Hornachos *E* **50** A2
Hornachuelos *E* **50** B3
Hornos *E* **53** B4
Hortezuela *E* **33** B6
Hortigüela *E* **25** D5
Hostalric *E* **37** B5
Hoya Gonzalo *E* **43** D5
Hoyocasero *E* **32** D3
Hoyo de Manzanares *E* **33** D5
Hoyos *E* **39** A6
Hoyos del Espino *E* **32** D2

Huarte *E* **26** C3
Huécija *E* **53** D4
Huélago *E* **52** C3
Huelma *E* **52** C3
Huelva *E* **49** D6
Huelves *E* **42** A2
Huércal de Almería *E* **59** B5
Huércal-Overa *E* **53** C5
Huérguina *E* **43** A4
Huérmeces *E* **25** C5
Huerta del Marquesada *E* **43** A4
Huerta del Rey *E* **33** A5
Huerta de Valdecarábanos *E* **41** B6
Huertahernando *E* **34** C2
Huerto *E* **35** A5
Huesa *E* **52** C3
Huesa del Común *E* **35** C4
Huesca *E* **27** D5
Huéscar *E* **53** C4
Huete *E* **42** A3
Huétor-Tájar *E* **51** D6
Huétor-Vega *E* **52** D2
Huévar *E* **50** C2
Humanes de Madrid *E* **41** A6
Humanes de Mohernando *E* **33** C6
Humilladero *E* **51** D4
Hurteles *E* **26** D2

I

Ibahernando *E* **40** C2
Ibarra *E* **26** B2
Ibdes *E* **34** C3
Ibeas de Juarros *E* **25** D5
Ibi *E* **43** D6
Ibiza *E* **45** D6
Ibros *E* **52** B3
Idanha-a-Nova *P* **39** B5
Idanha-a-Velha *P* **39** A5
Idiazabal *E* **26** B2
Idocin *E* **26** C3
Igea *E* **26** D2
Igorre *E* **25** B6
Igrejinha *P* **39** D4
Igualada *E* **36** B3
Igualeja *E* **57** B4
Igueña *E* **23** C6
Ílhavo *P* **30** D2
Illana *E* **42** A2
Illar *E* **53** D4
Illescas *E* **41** A6
Íllora *E* **51** D6
Illueca *E* **34** B3
Inca *E* **47** B4
Incinillas *E* **25** C5
Infiesto *E* **24** B2
Iniesta *E* **43** C4
Instinción *E* **53** D4
Irueste *E* **33** D6
Irún *E* **26** B3

Iruña *E* **26** C3
Irurita *E* **26** B3
Irurozqui *E* **27** C4
Irurtzun *E* **26** C3
Isaba *E* **27** C4
Íscar *E* **32** B3
Isla Cristina *E* **49** D5
Isla Plana *E* **54** C2
Isna *P* **39** B4
Isona *E* **28** D2
Isso *E* **53** A6
Istán *E* **57** B5
Isuerre *E* **27** C4
Itero de la Vega *E* **25** D4
Itrabo *E* **58** B2
Ituero de Azaba *E* **31** D5
Ivars d'Urgell *E* **36** B2
Izarra *E* **25** C6
Izeda *P* **31** B5
Iznájar *E* **51** D5
Iznalloz *E* **52** C3

J

Jabaga *E* **42** A3
Jabaloyas *E* **43** A5
Jabalquinto *E* **51** B6
Jabugo *E* **49** B6
Jaca *E* **27** C5
Jadraque *E* **33** C6
Jaén *E* **51** C6
Jalance *E* **43** C5
Jamilena *E* **51** C6
Jaraba *E* **34** C2
Jarafuel *E* **43** C5
Jaraicejo *E* **40** B2
Jaraíz de la Vera *E* **40** A2
Jarandilla de la Vera *E* **40** A2
Jarque *E* **34** B3
Jatar *E* **51** D6
Játiva *E* **43** D6
Jaulín *E* **35** B4
Jauntsarats *E* **26** B3
Jaurrieta *E* **27** C4
Javalí Viejo *E* **54** B2
Jávea-Xábia *E* **44** D3
Javier *E* **27** C4
Jayena *E* **51** D6
Jédula *E* **56** B3
Jerez de la Frontera *E* **56** B3
Jerez del Marquesado *E* **52** D3
Jerez de los Caballeros *E* **49** A6
Jérica *E* **43** B6
Jerte *E* **40** A2
Jijona-Xixona *E* **55** A4
Jimena *E* **52** C3
Jimena de la Frontera *E* **57** B4
Joane *P* **30** B2
Jódar *E* **52** C3
Jolda *P* **30** A2
Jorba *E* **36** B3

Jorcas *E* **35** D4
Jorquera *E* **43** C5
Jou *P* **31** B4
Jubrique *E* **57** B4
Jumilla *E* **54** A2
Juncal *P* **38** B2
Juncosa *E* **36** B1
Juneda *E* **36** B2
Junqueira *P* **49** D5

K

Krutzea *E* **25** B6

L

La Adrada *E* **41** A4
La Alberca *E* **31** D6
La Alberca *E* **54** B3
La Alberca de Záncara *E* **42** C3
La Alberguería de Argañán *E* **31** D5
La Albuera *E* **39** D6
La Aldehuela *E* **32** D2
La Algaba *E* **50** C2
La Aliseda de Tormes *E* **32** D2
La Aljorra *E* **54** C3
La Almarcha *E* **42** B3
La Almolda *E* **35** B5
La Almunia de Doña Godina *E* **34** B3
La Antilla *E* **49** D5
La Azohía *E* **54** C3
Labajos *E* **32** C3
La Bañeza *E* **23** D6
La Bisbal de Falset *E* **36** B1
La Bisbal del Penedès *E* **36** B3
La Bisbal d'Empordà *E* **37** A5
La Bóveda de Toro *E* **32** B2
La Cabrera *E* **33** C5
Lacalahorra *E* **52** D3
La Calzada de Oropesa *E* **40** B3
La Campana *E* **50** C3
La Cañada de San Urbano *E* **59** B5
La Cañada de Verich *E* **35** C6
La Caridad *E* **23** A5
La Carlota *E* **51** C4
La Carolina *E* **51** A6
La Cavada *E* **25** B5
La Cellera de Ter *E* **37** A5
La Cerca *E* **25** C5
La Cerollera *E* **35** C6
Lachar *E* **51** D6
La Cierva *E* **43** A4
La Cisterniga *E* **32** B3
La Codosera *E* **39** C5
La Concha *E* **25** B5

La Coronada *E* **40** D2
La Coronada *E* **50** B3
La Coruña *E* **22** B2
La Cumbre *E* **40** C2
Ladoeiro *P* **39** B5
La Encina *E* **43** D6
La Ercina *E* **24** C2
La Espina *E* **23** B6
La Estación *E* **37** A4
La Estrella *E* **40** B3
La Fatarrella *E* **36** C1
La Felipa *E* **43** D4
La Font de la Figuera *E* **43** D6
Lafortunada *E* **27** C6
La Fregeneda *E* **31** C5
La Fresneda *E* **35** C6
La Frontera *E* **34** D2
La Fuente de San Esteban *E* **31** C6
La Fuliola *E* **36** B2
La Galera *E* **35** D6
Lagarelhos *P* **31** B4
Lagares da Beira *P* **30** D3
La Garriga *E* **37** B4
La Garrovilla *E* **39** D6
La Gineta *E* **43** C4
Lagoa *P* **31** B5
Lagoa *P* **48** D3
Lagoaça *P* **31** C5
Lago Menor *E* **47** B4
La Gornal *E* **36** C3
Lagos *P* **48** D3
Lagran *E* **26** C1
La Granada de Riotinto *E* **49** C6
La Granadella *E* **36** B1
La Granja d'Escarp *E* **35** B6
La Granjuela *E* **50** A3
La Guarda *E* **40** D2
Laguardia *E* **26** C1
La Guardia *E* **30** A1
La Guardia *E* **41** B6
La Guardia de Jaén *E* **51** C6
Laguarta *E* **27** D5
Laguna Dalga *E* **24** D1
Laguna de Duero *E* **32** B3
Laguna de Negrillos *E* **24** D1
Lagunilla *E* **31** D6
La Haba *E* **40** D2
La Higuera *E* **43** D5
La Hiniesta *E* **32** B1
La Hinojosa *E* **42** B3
La Horcajada *E* **32** D2
La Horra *E* **33** A5
La Iglesuela *E* **41** A4
La Iglesuela del Cid *E* **35** D5
La Iruela *E* **53** B4
La Jana *E* **35** D6
Lajeosa *P* **31** D5
Lajeosa do Mondego *P* **31** D4
La Jonquera *E* **29** D5
Lakuntza *E* **26** C2

La Lantejuela *E* **51** C4
La Lapa *E* **49** A6
L'Albagés *E* **36** B1
L'Alcudia *E* **43** C6
L'Alcudia de Crespins *E* **43** D6
L'Alfàs del Pi *E* **55** A4
Lalín *E* **22** C3
La Línea de la Concepción *E* **57** C4
Lalueza *E* **35** A5
La Luisiana *E* **50** C3
La Magdalena *E* **24** C1
La Manga del Mar Menor *E* **54** C3
Lamas *P* **30** C2
La Massana *AND* **28** C3
La Mata *E* **41** B5
La Mata de los Olmos *E* **35** C5
La Matilla *E* **33** C5
Lamego *P* **30** C3
Lameiras *P* **31** D4
L'Ametlla de Mar *E* **36** C2
Lamiaco *E* **25** B6
Lamiako *E* **25** B6
La Mojonera *E* **59** B4
La Morera *E* **49** A6
La Mudarra *E* **32** A3
La Muela *E* **35** B4
Lanaja *E* **35** A5
La Nava *E* **49** B6
La Nava de Ricomalillo *E* **41** B4
La Nava de Santiago *E* **39** C6
Landete *E* **43** B5
Langa *E* **32** C3
Langa de Duero *E* **33** B5
Langraiz Oka *E* **25** C6
Langreo *E* **24** B1
Languilla *E* **33** B5
Lanjarón *E* **52** D3
Lantadilla *E* **25** D4
La Nucía *E* **55** A4
Lanzahita *E* **41** A4
La Paca *E* **53** B6
La Palma *E* **54** C3
La Palma del Condado *E* **49** C6
La Parra *E* **49** A6
La Parra de Las Vegas *E* **42** B3
La Peraleja *E* **42** A3
La Pesga *E* **31** D6
La Peza *E* **52** D3
La Pinilla *E* **54** C2
La Plaza *E* **23** B6
La Pobla de Claramunt *E* **36** B3
La Pobla del Duc *E* **44** D2
La Pobla de Lillet *E* **29** D4
La Pobla de Montornès *E* **36** C3
La Pobla de Segur *E* **28** D2

La Pobla de Vallbona *E* **43** B6
La Pola de Gordón *E* **24** C2
La Portellada *E* **35** C6
La Portera *E* **43** C5
La Proveda de Soria *E* **26** D1
La Puebla *E* **47** B4
La Puebla de Almoradiel *E* **42** B2
La Puebla de Arganzón *E* **25** C6
La Puebla de Cazalla *E* **50** D3
La Puebla de los Infantes *E* **50** C3
La Puebla del Río *E* **50** D2
La Puebla de Montalbán *E* **41** B5
La Puebla de Valdavia *E* **24** C3
La Puebla de Valverde *E* **43** A6
La Puerta de Segura *E* **53** A4
Laracha *E* **22** B2
La Rambla *E* **51** C4
Laranueva *E* **34** C1
La Rasa *E* **33** B6
L'Arboç *E* **36** C3
Lardero *E* **26** D2
Laredo *E* **25** B5
La Riba *E* **36** B2
La Riba de Escalote *E* **33** B6
La Rinconada *E* **50** C2
L'Armentera *E* **29** D5
La Robla *E* **24** C2
La Roca de la Sierra *E* **39** C6
La Roda *E* **42** C3
La Roda de Andalucía *E* **51** D4
Laroles *E* **53** D4
La Romana *E* **54** A3
Larraga *E* **26** C3
Larrasoaina *E* **26** C3
Larrión *E* **26** C2
Larva *E* **52** C3
Las Arenas *E* **24** B3
La Savina *E* **45** D6
Las Berlanas *E* **32** C3
Las Cabezas de San Juan *E* **50** D2
Las Casas *E* **44** B3
Lascuarre *E* **28** D1
La Seca *E* **32** B3
La Secuita *E* **36** C2
La Selva del Camp *E* **36** C2
La Sènia *E* **35** D6
Las Herencias *E* **41** B4
Las Labores *E* **41** C6
Las Majadas *E* **43** A4
Las Menas *E* **53** D4
Las Mesas *E* **42** C2
Las Navas de la Concepción *E* **50** B3
Las Navas del Marqués *E* **33** D4

Las Negras *E* **59** A5
La Solana *E* **42** D2
Las Palas *E* **54** C2
Las Pedroñeras *E* **42** C3
Las Pedrosas *E* **27** D4
Las Rotas *E* **44** D3
Las Rozas de Madrid *E* **33** D5
Las Terreras *E* **53** B6
Las Torres de Cotillas *E* **54** B2
Lastras de Cuéllar *E* **33** B4
Las Veguillas *E* **32** D1
Las Ventas con Peña Aguilera *E* **41** B5
Las Ventas de San Julián *E* **40** A3
La Torre de Cabdella *E* **28** D2
La Torre de Esteban Hambrán *E* **41** A5
La Torre de l'Espanyol *E* **36** C1
Laudio *E* **25** B6
Laujar de Andarax *E* **53** D4
La Unión *E* **54** C3
La Vecilla *E* **24** C2
La Vega *E* **23** B6
La Vega *E* **24** B2
La Vega *E* **24** B3
La Vellés *E* **32** C2
La Ventosa *E* **42** A3
La Victoria *E* **51** C4
La Vid *E* **33** B5
La Villa de Don Fadrique *E* **42** B2
Lavradio *P* **38** D2
Lavre *P* **38** D3
Laxe *E* **22** B1
Layana *E* **27** D4
La Yesa *E* **43** B6
Layos *E* **41** B5
Laza *E* **31** A4
Lazagurría *E* **26** C2
Lazkao *E* **26** B2
Lebrija *E* **50** D2
Lebução *P* **31** A4
Leça da Palmeira *P* **30** C2
Leça do Bailio *P* **30** C2
Lécera *E* **35** C4
Leciñena *E* **35** A5
Lecrín *E* **52** D3
Ledaña *E* **43** C4
Ledanca *E* **33** C6
Ledesma *E* **31** C6
Ledigos *E* **24** D3
Ledrada *E* **32** D1
Leganés *E* **41** A6
Leganiel *E* **42** A2
Legazpi *E* **26** B2
Legutiano *E* **26** B1
Leirado *E* **22** D3
Leiria *P* **38** B2
Leiro *E* **22** D3
Leitza *E* **26** B2

Lekunberri *E* **26** B3
León *E* **24** C2
Lepe *E* **49** D5
Lérida *E* **36** B1
Lerín *E* **26** C2
Lerma *E* **25** D5
Lesaka *E* **26** B3
Les Avellanes *E* **36** A1
Les Borges Blanques *E* **36** B2
Les Borges del Camp *E* **36** C2
L'Escala *E* **29** D5
Les Cases d'Alcanar *E* **36** D1
Les Escaldes *AND* **28** C3
Le Seu d'Urgell *E* **28** D3
Les Planes d'Hostoles *E* **29** D5
L'Espluga Calba *E* **36** B2
L'Espluga de Francolí *E* **36** B2
Les Preses *E* **29** D4
Les Useres *E* **44** A3
Letur *E* **53** A5
Lezuza *E* **42** D3
L'Hospitalet de l'Infant *E* **36** C2
L'Hospitalet de Llobregat *E* **37** B4
L'Hostal del Alls *E* **36** D1
Librilla *E* **54** B2
Libros *E* **43** A5
Liceras *E* **33** B6
Liédena *E* **27** C4
Liétor *E* **53** A5
Lijar *E* **53** D5
Lillo *E* **42** B1
Limpias *E* **25** B5
Linares *E* **51** B6
Linares de Mora *E* **43** A6
Linares de Riofrío *E* **31** D6
Lindoso *P* **30** A3
Linhares *P* **31** D4
Lintzoain *E* **26** B3
Linyola *E* **36** B2
Lisboa *P* **38** D2
Lisbon *P* **38** D2
Lizarra *E* **26** C2
Lizarraga *E* **26** C2
Llagostera *E* **37** A5
Llamas de la Ribera *E* **24** C1
Llança *E* **29** D6
Llanes *E* **24** B3
Llardecans *E* **36** B1
Llauri *E* **44** C2
Llavorsí *E* **28** C2
Lleida *E* **36** B1
Llera *E* **50** A2
Llerena *E* **50** B2
Lliria *E* **43** B6
Llívia *E* **29** D4
Llodio *E* **25** B6
Llombai *E* **43** C6
Lloret de Mar *E* **37** B5
Lloseta *E* **47** B4

Llubí *E* **47** B4
Lluchmayor *E* **47** C4
Llucmajor *E* **47** C4
Loarre *E* **27** D5
Lobera de Onsella *E* **27** C4
Lobón *E* **39** D6
Lodosa *E* **26** D2
Loeches *E* **33** D5
Logroño *E* **26** D2
Logrosán *E* **40** C3
Loivos *P* **31** B4
Loivos do Monte *P* **30** C3
Loja *E* **51** D5
L'Ollería *E* **43** D6
Longares *E* **35** B4
Longomel *P* **39** C4
Longos Vales *P* **30** A2
Longroiva *P* **31** C4
Lopera *E* **51** B5
Lora del Río *E* **50** C3
Loranca de Tajuña *E* **33** D6
Lorca *E* **53** C6
Lorcha *E* **44** D2
Lordelo *P* **30** B3
Lordosa *P* **30** D3
Loriguilla *E* **43** B6
Losacino *E* **31** B6
Losa del Obispo *E* **43** B6
Los Alcázares *E* **54** C3
Los Algezares *E* **54** B3
Los Arcos *E* **26** C2
Losar de la Vera *E* **40** A3
Los Arenales del Sol *E* **55** B4
Los Barrios *E* **57** C4
Los Barrios de Luna *E* **23** C6
Los Belones *E* **54** C3
Los Cantareros *E* **53** C6
Los Corrales *E* **51** D4
Los Corrales de Buelna *E* **25** B4
Loscos *E* **35** C4
Los Dolores *E* **54** C3
Los Gallardos *E* **53** D5
Los Hinojosos *E* **42** B2
Los Maldonados *E* **54** C2
Los Molinos *E* **33** D4
Los Navalmorales *E* **41** B4
Los Navalucillos *E* **41** B4
Los Palacios y Villafranca *E* **50** D2
Los Pandos *E* **25** B4
Los Pedrones *E* **43** C5
Los Pozuelos de Calatrava *E* **41** D6
Los Rábanos *E* **34** B2
Los Royos *E* **53** B5
Los Santos *E* **32** D1
Los Santos de Maimona *E* **50** A1
Los Tojos *E* **25** B4
Los Villares *E* **51** C6
Los Yébenes *E* **41** B6
Loulé *E* **49** D4
Lourical *P* **38** A2
Lourinhã *P* **38** C1

Lousã *P* **38** A3
Lousa *P* **38** D2
Lousada *P* **30** B2
Lozoya *E* **33** C5
Lozoyuela *E* **33** C5
Luanco *E* **24** A1
Luarca *E* **23** A5
Lubián *E* **31** A5
Lubrín *E* **53** D5
Lucainena de las Torres *E* **53** D5
Lúcar *E* **53** C5
Lucena *E* **51** C5
Lucena de Jalón *E* **35** B4
Lucena del Cid *E* **44** A2
Lucena del Puerto *E* **49** D6
Luceni *E* **35** A4
Luciana *E* **41** D5
Lucillo de Somoza *E* **23** D6
Luelmo *E* **31** B6
Luesia *E* **27** D4
Lugo *E* **23** C4
Lugones *E* **24** B1
Lugros *E* **52** D3
Luintra *E* **22** D3
Lumbier *E* **26** C3
Lumbrales *E* **31** C5
Lumbreras *E* **26** D1
Lumpiaque *E* **34** B3
Luna *E* **27** D4
Lupiñén *E* **27** D5
Lupión *E* **52** B3
Luso *P* **30** D2
Luyego de Somoza *E* **23** D6
Luz *P* **48** D2
Luz *P* **49** A5
Luz *P* **49** D4
Luzaga *E* **34** C2
Luzianes *P* **48** C3
Luzmela *E* **25** B4
Luzón *E* **34** C2

M

Macael *E* **53** D5
Maçanet de Cabrenys *E* **29** D5
Maçanet de la Selva *E* **37** A5
Mação *P* **39** B4
Macastre *E* **43** C6
Maceda *E* **23** D4
Maceda *P* **30** C2
Macedo de Cavaleiros *P* **31** B5
Maceira *P* **31** D4
Maceira *P* **38** B2
Machados *P* **49** B5
Macotera *E* **32** C2
Madrid *E* **33** D5
Madridejos *E* **41** C6
Madrigal de las Altas Torres *E* **32** C3
Madrigal de la Vera *E* **40** A3

Madrigal del Monte *E* **25** D5
Madrigalejo *E* **40** C3
Madrigueras *E* **43** C4
Madroñera *E* **40** C2
Maella *E* **35** C6
Maello *E* **32** C3
Mafra *P* **38** D1
Magacela *E* **40** D2
Magallón *E* **34** A3
Magalluf *E* **46** C3
Magaña *E* **34** A2
Magaz *E* **33** A4
Magueija *P* **30** C3
Maguilla *E* **50** A2
Mahíde *E* **31** A6
Mahón *E* **47** B6
Mahora *E* **43** C4
Maia *P* **30** C2
Maials *E* **36** B1
Maiorca *P* **38** A2
Maiorga *P* **38** B2
Mairena del Alcor *E* **50** C3
Majadahonda *E* **33** D5
Majadas de Tiétar *E* **40** B2
Malá *E* **51** D6
Málaga *E* **57** B6
Malagón *E* **41** C6
Malcocinado *E* **50** B3
Maleján *E* **34** A3
Malgrat de Mar *E* **37** B5
Malhadas *P* **31** B6
Mallén *E* **34** A3
Malón *E* **34** A3
Malpartida *P* **31** D5
Malpartida de Cáceres *E* **39** C6
Malpartida de la Serena *E* **40** D2
Malpartida de Plasencia *E* **40** B2
Malpica *E* **22** B2
Malpica de Tajo *E* **41** B4
Malpica do Tejo *P* **39** B5
Malta *P* **31** D4
Maluenda *E* **34** B3
Malva *E* **32** B2
Malveira *P* **38** D2
Mamarrosa *P* **30** D2
Mambrilla de Castejón *E* **33** B4
Manacor *E* **47** B4
Mañaria *E* **25** B6
Mancera de Abajo *E* **32** C2
Mancha Real *E* **51** C6
Manchita *E* **40** D2
Mandayona *E* **33** C6
Mañeru *E* **26** C3
Manganeses de la Lampreana *E* **32** A1
Manganeses de la Polvorosa *E* **24** D1
Mangualde *P* **30** D3
Manilva *E* **57** C4
Manises *E* **43** C6
Manlleu *E* **29** D4

Manresa *E* **36** B3
Mansilla *E* **25** D6
Mansilla de las Mulas *E* **24** D2
Mansores *P* **30** C2
Manteigas *P* **31** D4
Manuel *E* **43** D6
Manzanal de Arriba *E* **31** A6
Manzanal del Puerto *E* **23** C6
Manzanares *E* **42** D1
Manzanares el Real *E* **33** D5
Manzaneda *E* **23** D4
Manzanedo *E* **25** C5
Manzaneque *E* **41** B6
Manzanera *E* **43** A6
Manzanilla *E* **50** C1
Maó *E* **47** B6
Maqueda *E* **41** A5
Mar *P* **30** B2
Maranchón *E* **34** C2
Maranhão *P* **39** D4
Marateca *P* **38** D3
Marbella *E* **57** B5
Marça *E* **36** C2
Marchamalo *E* **33** D6
Marchena *E* **50** D3
Marcilla *E* **26** D3
Marco de Canaveses *P* **30** C3
María *E* **53** C5
Marialva *P* **31** C4
Mariana *E* **43** A4
Marín *E* **22** D2
Marinaleda *E* **51** C4
Marines *E* **43** B6
Marinha das Ondas *P* **38** A2
Marinha Grande *P* **38** B2
Marinhas *P* **30** B2
Marjaliza *E* **41** B5
Markina-Xemein *E* **26** B2
Marmelar *P* **49** B4
Marmeleira *P* **38** C2
Marmelete *P* **48** D3
Marmolejo *E* **51** B5
Martiago *E* **31** D6
Martiherrero *E* **32** D3
Martim Longo *P* **49** C4
Martinchel *P* **38** B3
Martín de la Jara *E* **51** D4
Martín del Río *E* **35** C4
Martín de Yeltes *E* **31** C6
Martinet *E* **28** D3
Martingança *P* **38** B2
Martín Muñoz de las Posadas *E* **32** C3
Martinporra *E* **24** B2
Martorell *E* **36** B3
Martos *E* **51** C6
Marugán *E* **33** C4
Marvão *P* **39** C5
Masa *E* **25** C5
Masalavés *E* **43** C6
Mascaraque *E* **41** B6
Mascarenhas *P* **31** B4

Mas de Barberans *E* **35** D6
Mas de las Matas *E* **35** C5
Masegosa *E* **34** D2
Masegoso *E* **42** D3
Masegoso de Tajuña *E* **34** C1
Maside *E* **22** D3
Masquefa *E* **36** B3
Massamagrell *E* **44** B2
Matabuena *E* **33** C5
Matadepera *E* **37** B4
Matalascañas *E* **49** D6
Matalebreras *E* **34** A2
Matallana de Valmadrigal *E* **24** D2
Matamala de Almazán *E* **34** B1
Matamorosa *E* **25** B4
Mataporquera *E* **25** C4
Matapozuelos *E* **32** B3
Mataró *E* **37** B4
Matosinhos *P* **30** C2
Maxial *P* **38** C2
Maxieira *P* **39** B4
Mayorga *E* **24** D2
Mazagón *E* **49** D6
Mazaleón *E* **35** C6
Mazarambroz *E* **41** B5
Mazarete *E* **34** C2
Mazarrón *E* **54** C2
Meadela *P* **30** B2
Mealhada *P* **30** D2
Mecina-Bombarón *E* **52** D3
Meco *E* **33** D6
Meda *P* **31** C4
Medelim *P* **39** A5
Medellín *E* **40** D2
Mediana *E* **35** B4
Medinaceli *E* **34** C2
Medina de las Torres *E* **50** A1
Medina del Campo *E* **32** B3
Medina de Pomar *E* **25** C5
Medina de Rioseco *E* **32** A3
Medina-Sidonia *E* **56** B3
Medinilla *E* **32** D2
Mediona *E* **36** B3
Meimoa *P* **39** A5
Meira *E* **23** B4
Mejorada *E* **41** A4
Mejorada del Campo *E* **33** D5
Melgaço *P* **22** D3
Melgar de Arriba *E* **24** D2
Melgar de Fernamental *E* **25** D4
Melgar de Tera *E* **31** A6
Meliana *E* **44** C2
Mélida *E* **26** D3
Melide *E* **22** C3
Melides *P* **48** B2
Melón *E* **22** D3
Melres *P* **30** C2
Membrilla *E* **42** D1
Membrío *E* **39** B5
Menasalbas *E* **41** B5
Mendaro *E* **26** B2

Mendavia *E* **26** D2
Mendiga *P* **38** C2
Mendigorría *E* **26** C3
Mengabril *E* **40** D2
Mengíbar *E* **51** B6
Méntrida *E* **41** A5
Mequinenza *E* **35** B6
Mercadal *E* **47** B6
Mercadillo *E* **25** B6
Mérida *E* **40** D1
Mértola *P* **49** C4
Mesão Frio *P* **30** C3
Messejana *P* **48** B3
Mestanza *E* **51** A6
Mezio *P* **30** C3
Mezquita de Jarque *E* **35** D4
Miajadas *E* **40** C2
Miedes *E* **34** C3
Mieres *E* **24** B1
Mieres *E* **29** D5
Mieza *E* **31** C5
Miguel Esteban *E* **42** C2
Miguelturra *E* **41** D6
Mijares *E* **41** A4
Mijas *E* **57** B5
Milagro *E* **26** D3
Milagros *E* **33** B5
Milfontes *P* **48** C2
Milhão *P* **31** A5
Millares *E* **43** C6
Milmarcos *E* **34** C2
Mimetiz *E* **25** B6
Mina de São Domingos *P* **49** C5
Minas de Riotinto *E* **49** C6
Minateda *E* **53** A6
Minaya *E* **42** C3
Minde *P* **38** C3
Minglanilla *E* **43** C5
Mingorría *E* **32** D3
Mira *E* **43** B5
Mira *P* **30** D2
Mirabel *E* **40** B1
Miraflores de la Sierra *E* **33** C5
Miralcamp *E* **36** B2
Mirambel *E* **35** D5
Miranda de Arga *E* **26** C3
Miranda de Ebro *E* **25** C6
Miranda do Corvo *P* **38** A3
Miranda do Douro *P* **31** B6
Mirandela *E* **31** B4
Mirandilla *E* **40** D1
Miravet *E* **36** C1
Miravete de la Sierra *E* **35** D5
Mirueña de los Infanzones *E* **32** D2
Moaña *E* **22** D2
Moçarria *P* **38** C2
Mocejón *E* **41** B6
Mochales *E* **34** C2
Moclín *E* **51** C6
Moclinejo *E* **57** B6
Mofreita *P* **31** A5

Mogadouro *P* **31** B5
Mogón *E* **52** B3
Moguer *E* **49** D6
Moharque *E* **53** A6
Mohedas de Granadilla *E* **40** A2
Mohedas de la Jara *E* **40** B3
Mohernando *E* **33** C6
Moià *E* **37** A4
Moimenta da Beira *P* **31** C4
Moita *P* **30** D2
Moita *P* **38** B2
Moita *P* **38** D2
Moixent-Mogente *E* **43** D6
Mojácar *E* **53** D6
Mojados *E* **32** B3
Molares *P* **30** B3
Moledo *P* **30** A1
Moledo *P* **30** C3
Molelos *P* **30** D3
Molina de Aragón *E* **34** C2
Molina de Segura *E* **54** B2
Molinar *E* **25** B6
Molinaseca *E* **23** D5
Molinicos *E* **53** A5
Molino de Villobas *E* **27** D5
Molinos *E* **35** C5
Molins de Rei *E* **37** B4
Molledo *E* **25** B4
Mollerussa *E* **36** B2
Mollet del Vallès *E* **37** B4
Molló *E* **29** D4
Molvízar *E* **58** B2
Mombeltrán *E* **41** A4
Mombuey *E* **31** A6
Monachil *E* **52** D3
Moncada *E* **44** C2
Monção *P* **22** D2
Moncarapacho *P* **49** D4
Monchique *P* **48** D3
Moncófar *E* **44** B3
Monda *E* **57** B5
Mondariz *E* **22** D2
Mondariz-Balneario *E* **22** D2
Mondéjar *E* **33** D6
Mondoñedo *E* **23** B4
Mondragón-Arrasate *E* **26** B2
Monegrillo *E* **35** B5
Monesterio *E* **50** B2
Monforte *E* **23** D4
Monforte *P* **39** C5
Monforte da Beira *P* **39** B5
Monforte del Cid *E* **54** A3
Monforte de Moyuela *E* **35** C4
Monfortinho *P* **39** A6
Monistrol de Calders *E* **37** A4
Monistrol de Montserrat *E* **36** B3
Monóvar *E* **54** A3
Monover *E* **54** A3
Monreal *E* **26** C3
Monreal del Campo *E* **34** D3

Monroy *E* **40** B1
Monroyo *E* **35** D6
Monsaraz *P* **49** A5
Monserrat *E* **43** C6
Montaberner *E* **43** D6
Montalbán *E* **35** C4
Montalbán de Córdoba *E* **51** C4
Montalbo *E* **42** B3
Montalegre *P* **30** A3
Montalvão *P* **39** B5
Montamarta *E* **32** B1
Montanejos *E* **43** A6
Montargil *P* **38** C3
Montblanc *E* **36** B2
Montbrió del Camp *E* **36** C2
Montcada i Reixac *E* **37** B4
Monteagudo *E* **34** A3
Monteagudo de las Salinas *E* **43** B4
Monteagudo de las Vicarías *E* **34** B2
Montealegre del Castillo *E* **43** D5
Monte da Pedra *P* **39** C4
Monte das Flores *P* **49** A4
Montederramo *E* **23** D4
Monte do Trigo *P* **49** A4
Montefrío *E* **51** D6
Monte Gordo *P* **49** D5
Montehermoso *E* **40** A1
Montejaque *E* **57** B4
Montejícar *E* **52** C3
Montejo de la Sierra *E* **33** C5
Montelavar *P* **38** D1
Montellano *E* **50** D3
Montemayor *E* **51** C4
Montemayor de Pililla *E* **33** B4
Montemolín *E* **50** B2
Montemor-o-Novo *P* **38** D3
Montenegro de Cameros *E* **25** D6
Monte Real *P* **38** B2
Monte Redondo *P* **38** B2
Monterrei *E* **31** A4
Monterroso *E* **22** C3
Monterrubio de la Serena *E* **40** D3
Montesa *E* **43** D6
Montesclaros *E* **41** A4
Montes Velhos *P* **48** B3
Montevil *P* **48** A3
Montgai *E* **36** A2
Montiel *E* **42** D2
Montijo *E* **39** D6
Montijo *P* **38** D2
Montilla *E* **51** C5
Montillana *E* **51** C6
Montizón *E* **52** A3
Montmelo *E* **37** B4
Montoito *P* **49** A4
Montón *E* **34** C3
Montoro *E* **51** B5
Mont-ras *E* **37** A5

Mont-roig del Camp *E* **36** C2
Montroy *E* **43** C6
Montseny *E* **37** A4
Montuïri *E* **47** B4
Monzón *E* **35** A6
Monzón de Campos *E* **24** D3
Mora *E* **41** B6
Mora *P* **38** D3
Mora de Rubielos *E* **43** A6
Moradillo de Roa *E* **33** B5
Moraira *E* **44** D3
Morais *P* **31** B5
Móra la Nova *E* **36** C1
Moral de Calatrava *E* **41** D6
Moraleda de Zafayona *E* **51** D6
Moraleja *E* **39** A6
Moraleja del Vino *E* **32** B2
Moraleja de Sayago *E* **31** C6
Morales de Campos *E* **32** A2
Morales del Vino *E* **32** B1
Morales de Toro *E* **32** B2
Morales de Valverde *E* **31** A6
Moralina *E* **31** B6
Morasverdes *E* **31** D6
Morata de Jalón *E* **34** B3
Morata de Tajuña *E* **41** A6
Moratalla *E* **53** B6
Moreanes *P* **49** C5
Moreda *E* **24** B1
Moreda *E* **52** C3
Morella *E* **35** D6
Morentín *E* **26** C2
Moreruela de Tábara *E* **32** A1
Moriles *E* **51** C4
Morón de Almazán *E* **34** B2
Morón de la Frontera *E* **50** D3
Moros *E* **34** B3
Mortágua *P* **30** D3
Moscavide *P* **38** D2
Mosqueruela *E* **35** D5
Mosteiro *E* **23** B4
Mosteiro *P* **39** B4
Mosteiro *E* **49** C4
Móstoles *E* **33** D5
Mota del Cuervo *E* **42** C2
Mota del Marqués *E* **32** B2
Motilla del Palancar *E* **43** B4
Motilleja *E* **43** C4
Motril *E* **58** B3
Moura *P* **49** B5
Mourão *P* **49** A5
Mourisca do Vouga *P* **30** D2
Mouriscas *P* **39** C4
Moya *E* **43** B5
Mozárbez *E* **32** C2
Mozelos *P* **30** D3
Mozoncillo *E* **33** C4
Mucientes *E* **32** A3
Muel *E* **35** B4
Muelas del Pan *E* **31** B6
Muga de Sayago *E* **31** B6
Mugardos *E* **22** B3

Muge *P* **38** C2
Muiños *E* **30** A3
Mula *E* **53** B6
Muñana *E* **32** D3
Mundaka *E* **25** B6
Munebrega *E* **34** C3
Munera *E* **42** D3
Mungia *E* **25** B6
Munguía *E* **25** B6
Muñico *E* **32** D3
Muniesa *E* **35** C4
Munilla *E* **26** D2
Muñogalindo *E* **32** D3
Muras *E* **22** B3
Murça *P* **31** B4
Murchante *E* **26** D3
Murcia *E* **54** B3
Murgia *E* **25** C6
Murias de Paredes *E* **23** C6
Muriedas *E* **25** B5
Murillo de Río Leza *E* **26** D2
Murillo el Fruto *E* **26** D3
Muro *E* **47** B4
Muro *P* **30** B2
Muro de Alcoy *E* **44** D2
Muros *E* **22** C1
Muros *E* **23** A6
Murtas *E* **58** A3
Murtede *P* **30** D2
Murueta *E* **25** B6
Mutiloa Baja *E* **26** C3
Mutriku *E* **26** B2
Mutxamel *E* **55** A4
Muxía *E* **22** B1

N

Nagore *E* **26** C3
Naharros *E* **42** A3
Nájera *E* **25** D6
Nalda *E* **26** D2
Nambroca *E* **41** B5
Náquera *E* **44** B2
Nava *E* **24** B2
Navacepeda de Tormes *E* **32** D2
Navaconcejo *E* **40** A2
Nava de Arévalo *E* **32** C3
Nava de la Asunción *E* **32** C3
Nava del Rey *E* **32** B2
Nava de Sotrobal *E* **32** C2
Navafría *E* **33** C5
Navahermosa *E* **41** B5
Navajas *E* **43** B6
Naval *E* **27** D6
Navalagamella *E* **33** D4
Navalcaballo *E* **34** B1
Navalcán *E* **40** A3
Navalcarnero *E* **41** A5
Navalero *E* **33** A6
Navalmanzano *E* **33** C4
Navalmoral *E* **32** D3
Navalmoral de la Mata *E* **40** B3

Navalonguilla *E* **40** A3
Navalosa *E* **32** D3
Navalperal de Pinares *E* **33** D4
Navalpino *E* **41** C4
Navaluenga *E* **32** D3
Navalvillar de Ibor *E* **40** B3
Navalvillar de Pela *E* **40** C3
Navamorcuende *E* **41** A4
Navarcles *E* **36** A3
Navardún *E* **27** C4
Navarredonda de la Rinconada *E* **31** D6
Navarrés *E* **43** C6
Navarrete *E* **26** D1
Navarrevisca *E* **32** D3
Navàs *E* **36** A3
Navascués *E* **27** C4
Navas de Estrena *E* **41** C4
Navas de Jorquera *E* **43** C4
Navas del Madroño *E* **39** B6
Navas del Rey *E* **33** D4
Navas de Oro *E* **33** C4
Navas de San Juan *E* **52** B3
Navasfrías *E* **39** A6
Navata *E* **29** D5
Navatalgordo *E* **32** D3
Nave *P* **48** D3
Nave de Haver *P* **31** D5
Nave Redonda *P* **48** C3
Navès *E* **36** A3
Navezuelas *E* **40** C3
Navia *E* **23** A5
Nazaré *P* **38** B2
Nebreda *E* **33** A5
Neda *E* **22** B3
Negredo *E* **33** C6
Negreira *E* **22** C2
Nelas *P* **30** D3
Nerja *E* **58** B2
Nerpio *E* **53** B5
Nerva *E* **49** C6
Niebla *E* **49** C6
Nigrán *E* **22** D2
Nigüelas *E* **52** D3
Níjar *E* **53** D5
Nisa *P* **39** C4
Noain *E* **26** C3
Noalejo *E* **51** C6
Noblejas *E* **41** B6
Noez *E* **41** B5
Nofuentes *E* **25** C5
Nogales *E* **39** D6
Nograles *E* **33** B6
Noguera *E* **34** D3
Nogueruelas *E* **43** A6
Noia *E* **22** C1
Noja *E* **25** A5
Nombela *E* **41** A4
Nonaspe *E* **35** C6
Noreña *E* **24** B1
Nossa Senhora da Boa Fé *P* **49** A4
Nossa Senhora da Graça de Póvoa e Meadas *P* **39** C5

Nossa Senhora da Graça do Divor *P* **39** D4
Nossa Senhora da Graça dos Degolados *P* **39** C5
Nossa Senhora das Neves *P* **49** B4
Nossa Senhora de Machede *P* **39** D4
Novales *E* **25** B4
Novales *E* **27** D5
Novallas *E* **34** A3
Novelda *E* **54** A3
Novés *E* **41** A5
Noviergas *E* **34** B2
Noya *E* **22** C1
Nubledo *E* **23** A6
Nueno *E* **27** D5
Nuestra Señora del Pilar *E* **45** D6
Nueva *E* **24** B3
Nueva-Carteya *E* **51** C5
Nueva Jarilla *E* **56** B3
Nuez de Ebro *E* **35** B4
Nules *E* **44** B3
Nuñomoral *E* **31** D6

O

O Arrabal *E* **30** A1
O Barco *E* **23** D5
Obejo *E* **51** B4
Óbidos *P* **38** C2
O Bolo *E* **23** D4
Obón *E* **35** C4
O Cádabo *E* **23** C4
O Campo da Feira *E* **22** B2
Ocaña *E* **41** B6
O Carballiño *E* **22** D3
O Castelo *E* **22** D2
O Castro *E* **22** C3
Ochagavía *E* **27** C4
O Convento *E* **22** D2
O Corgo *E* **23** C4
Odeceixe *P* **48** C2
Odeleite *P* **49** D5
Odelouca *P* **48** D3
Odemira *P* **48** C3
Òdena *E* **36** B3
Odiáxere *P* **48** D3
Odivelas *P* **38** D2
Odivelas *P* **48** B3
Odón *E* **34** C3
Oeiras *P* **38** D1
O Forte *E* **22** C2
O Grove *E* **22** D1
Ohanes *E* **53** D4
Oiã *P* **30** D2
O Igrexario *E* **22** D3
Oímbra *E* **31** A4
Oion *E* **26** C2
O Irixo *E* **22** D3
Ojén *E* **57** B5
Ojos Negros *E* **34** D3
Olague *E* **26** B3

Olalhas *P* **38** B3
Olave *E* **26** C3
Olazti *E* **26** C2
Olba *E* **43** A6
Oleiros *P* **39** B4
Olesa de Montserrat *E* **36** B3
Olhalvo *P* **38** C2
Olhão *P* **49** D4
Olho Marinho *P* **38** C2
Oliana *E* **28** D2
Olías del Rey *E* **41** B5
Oliete *E* **35** C5
Oliola *E* **36** A2
Olite *E* **26** C3
Oliva *E* **44** D3
Oliva de la Frontera *E* **49** A6
Oliva de Mérida *E* **40** D2
Olival *P* **38** B3
Olivares *E* **50** C2
Olivares de Júcar *E* **42** B3
Oliveira de Azeméis *P* **30** C2
Oliveira de Frades *P* **30** D3
Oliveira do Arda *P* **30** C2
Oliveira do Bairro *P* **30** D2
Oliveira do Conde *P* **30** D3
Oliveira do Douro *P* **30** C2
Oliveira do Hospital *P* **30** D3
Olivenza *E* **39** D5
Ollo *E* **26** C3
Olmedilla de Roa *E* **33** A4
Olmedo *E* **32** B3
Olmos de Ojeda *E* **25** C4
Olocau *E* **43** B6
Olocau del Rey *E* **35** D5
Olombrada *E* **33** B4
Olost *E* **37** A4
Olot *E* **29** D5
Olula del Río *E* **53** D5
Olvan *E* **28** D3
Ólvega *E* **34** A2
Olvena *E* **27** D6
Olvera *E* **50** D3
O Mesón do Vento *E* **22** B2
O Mosteiro *E* **22** D2
Oña *E* **25** C5
Oñati *E* **26** B2
Oncala *E* **34** A2
Onda *E* **44** B3
Ondara *E* **44** D3
Ondarroa *E* **26** B2
Onteniente *E* **43** D6
Ontiñena *E* **35** B6
Ontinyent *E* **43** D6
Ontur *E* **43** D5
Onzonilla *E* **24** C2
O Pazo *E* **22** D2
O Pazo de Irixoa *E* **22** B3
O Pedrouzo *E* **22** C2
O Porriño *E* **22** D2
Oporto *P* **30** C2
Orada *P* **39** D5
Orba *E* **44** D3
Orbacém *P* **30** A2
Orbara *E* **27** B4
Orca *P* **39** A5

Orce *E* **53** C4
Orcera *E* **53** A4
Órdenes *E* **22** B2
Ordes *E* **22** B2
Ordizia *E* **26** B2
Orduña *E* **25** B6
Orea *E* **34** D3
O Real *E* **22** B2
Orellana de la Sierra *E* **40** D3
Orellana la Vieja *E* **40** D3
Orense *E* **22** D3
Orés *E* **27** D4
Organyà *E* **28** D2
Orgaz *E* **41** B6
Orgiva *E* **58** A3
Oria *E* **53** C5
O Rial *E* **22** D2
Orihuela *E* **54** B3
Orihuela del Tremedal *E* **34** D3
Orio *E* **26** B2
Oriola *E* **49** A4
Oristà *E* **37** A4
Oronoz *E* **26** B3
Oropesa *E* **40** B3
Oropesa *E* **44** A3
Ororbia *E* **26** C3
Orreaga *E* **26** B3
Orrios *E* **35** D4
Ortigosa *E* **25** D6
Ortigueira *E* **22** A3
Orusco *E* **42** A2
Orvalho *P* **39** A4
Osa de Vega *E* **42** B2
Os Blancos *E* **30** A3
Os Dices *E* **22** C2
O Seixo *E* **30** A2
Oseja de Sajambre *E* **24** B3
Osera *E* **35** B5
Osma *E* **25** C6
Osor *E* **37** A5
Osorno *E* **25** D4
Ossa de Montiel *E* **42** D2
Ostiz *E* **26** C3
Osuna *E* **51** D4
Oteiza *E* **26** C2
Otero de Bodas *E* **31** A6
Otívar *E* **58** B2
O Toural *E* **22** D2
Otxandio *E* **26** B1
Ouca *P* **30** D2
Ouguela *E* **39** C5
Ourense *E* **22** D3
Ourique *P* **48** C3
Ourol *E* **23** A4
Outeiro *E* **30** A2
Outeiro *P* **31** B5
Outeiro de Rei *E* **23** B4
Outeiro Seco *E* **31** A4
Outomuro *E* **22** D3
Ovar *P* **30** C2
Oviedo *E* **23** B6
Oza *E* **22** B3
Ozeta *E* **26** C2

P

Pacos de Ferreira *P* **30** B2
Paderne *P* **22** D2
Paderne *P* **48** D3
Paderne de Allariz *E* **22** D3
Padrón *E* **22** C2
Padul *E* **51** D6
Paião *P* **38** A2
Pajares de la Lampreana *E* **32** B1
Pajarón *E* **43** B4
Palacios del Sil *E* **23** C5
Palacios de Sanabria *E* **31** A5
Palaciosrubios *E* **32** C2
Palafrugell *E* **37** A6
Palamós *E* **37** A5
Palas de Rei *E* **22** C3
Palencia *E* **32** A3
Palenciana *E* **51** D5
Palenzuela *E* **25** D4
Palhaça *P* **30** D2
Pallarés *E* **50** B2
Palma *P* **48** A3
Palma del Río *E* **50** C3
Palma de Mallorca *E* **46** B3
Palma Nova *E* **46** C3
Palmaz *P* **30** C2
Palmeira *P* **30** B2
Palmela *P* **38** D2
Palomar de Arroyos *E* **35** D4
Palomares del Río *E* **50** D2
Palomas *E* **40** D2
Palomera *E* **43** A4
Palomeras del Campo *E* **42** B3
Palos de la Frontera *E* **49** D6
Pals *E* **37** A6
Pampilhosa *P* **30** D2
Pampilhosa da Serra *P* **39** A4
Pampliega *E* **25** D4
Pamplona *E* **26** C3
Pancorbo *E* **25** C6
Pancrudo *E* **35** D4
Panes *E* **24** B3
Paniza *E* **35** B4
Panóias *P* **48** C3
Panticosa *E* **27** C5
Pantoja *E* **41** A6
Paracuellos *E* **43** B4
Paracuellos de Jarama *E* **33** D5
Parada *P* **31** D5
Parada de Ester *P* **30** C3
Parada de Pinhão *P* **31** B4
Parada de Rubiales *E* **32** C2
Parada de Sil *E* **23** D4
Paradas *E* **50** D3
Paradela *E* **23** C4
Paradela *P* **30** A3
Paradela *P* **31** C4
Parâmio *P* **31** A5
Páramo del Sil *E* **23** C5
Paranhos *P* **30** D3

Parcent *E* **44** D3
Pardais *P* **39** D5
Pardilhó *P* **30** C2
Paredes de Coura *P* **30** A2
Paredes de Nava *E* **24** D3
Pareja *E* **34** D1
Parets del Vallès *E* **37** B4
Parla *E* **41** A6
Parrillas *E* **41** A4
Partaloa *E* **53** C5
Pasai Donibane *E* **26** B2
Pasajes de San Juan *E* **26** B2
Pastoriza *E* **23** B4
Pastrana *E* **33** D6
Pataias *P* **38** B2
Paterna *E* **43** C6
Paterna del Campo *E* **50** C1
Paterna del Madera *E* **53** A5
Paterna del Río *E* **53** D4
Paterna de Rivera *E* **56** B3
Paül *P* **39** A4
Paüls *E* **35** C6
Pavia *P* **39** D4
Pavías *E* **43** B6
Paymogo *E* **49** C5
Pazos *E* **22** D2
Peal de Becerro *E* **52** B3
Pechina *E* **53** D5
Pedrafita do Cebreiro *E* **23** C5
Pedrajas de San Esteban *E* **32** B3
Pedralba *E* **43** B6
Pedralba de la Pradería *E* **31** A5
Pedraza de Campos *E* **32** A3
Pedrera *E* **51** D4
Pedro Abad *E* **51** B5
Pedro Bernardo *E* **41** A4
Pedroche *E* **51** A4
Pedrógão *P* **38** B2
Pedrógão *P* **39** A5
Pedrógão *P* **49** B4
Pedrógão Grande *P* **38** B3
Pedrógão Pequeno *P* **39** B4
Pedro-Martínez *E* **52** C3
Pedro Muñoz *E* **42** C2
Pedrosa *E* **25** B5
Pedrosa del Príncipe *E* **25** D4
Pedrosillo de los Aires *E* **32** D1
Pedroso *E* **25** D6
Pedroso *P* **30** C2
Pedrouzos *E* **22** C2
Pega *P* **31** D4
Pegalajar *E* **51** C6
Pego *E* **44** D3
Pego *P* **38** C3
Pegões *P* **38** D3
Peguera *E* **46** B3
Pelahustán *E* **41** A4
Pelarrodríguez *E* **31** C6
Peleagonzalo *E* **32** B2
Peloche *E* **40** C3
Peñacerrada *E* **25** C6

Penacova *P* **38** A3
Peñafiel *E* **33** B4
Penafiel *P* **30** C2
Peñaflor *E* **50** C3
Peñaflor de Hornija *E* **32** B3
Penagos *E* **25** B5
Peñalba *E* **35** B6
Peñalén *E* **34** D2
Peñalsordo *E* **40** D3
Penalva do Castelo *P* **30** D3
Penamacor *P* **39** A5
Peñaranda de Bracamonte *E* **32** C2
Peñaranda de Duero *E* **33** B5
Peñarroya de Tastavins *E* **35** D6
Peñarroya-Pueblonuevo *E* **50** A3
Peñarrubia *E* **53** A5
Peñascosa *E* **42** D3
Peñas de San Pedro *E* **43** D4
Peñausende *E* **32** B1
Pendilhe *P* **30** C3
Penedo Gordo *P* **49** B4
Penedono *P* **31** C4
Penela *P* **38** A3
Penha Garcia *P* **39** A5
Peniche *P* **38** C1
Peñíscola *E* **35** D6
Peque *E* **23** D6
Pêra *P* **48** D3
Perais *P* **39** B4
Peralada *E* **29** D5
Peraleda de la Mata *E* **40** B3
Peraleda del Zaucejo *E* **50** A3
Peralejos *E* **35** D4
Peralejos de las Truchas *E* **34** D2
Perales del Alfambra *E* **35** D4
Perales del Puerto *E* **39** A6
Peralta *E* **26** D3
Peralta de Alcofea *E* **35** A6
Peralta de la Sal *E* **27** D6
Peraltilla *E* **27** D6
Peralva *P* **49** D4
Peralveche *E* **34** D1
Peramola *E* **28** D2
Perdiguera *E* **35** B5
Peredo *P* **31** B5
Pereiras *P* **48** C3
Pereiro *E* **22** A3
Pereiro *P* **49** C5
Pereiro de Aguiar *E* **22** D3
Pereruela *E* **32** B1
Periana *E* **51** D5
Perilla de Castro *E* **32** B1
Pernes *P* **38** C2
Peroguarda *P* **49** B4
Pero Viseu *P* **39** A5
Pertusa *E* **27** D5
Pesadas de Burgos *E* **25** C5
Peso da Régua *P* **30** C3
Pesquera de Duero *E* **33** B4

Pesués *E* **24** B3
Petín *E* **23** D4
Petra *E* **47** B4
Petrel *E* **54** A3
Petrer *E* **54** A3
Pétrola *E* **43** D5
Pias *P* **49** B5
Picassent *E* **43** C6
Picón *E* **41** C5
Picoto *P* **30** C2
Piedrabuena *E* **41** D5
Piedrafita de Babia *E* **23** C6
Piedrahita *E* **32** D2
Piedralaves *E* **41** A4
Piedras Albas *E* **39** B6
Piedras Blancas *E* **23** A6
Piera *E* **36** B3
Pilas *E* **50** D2
Piles *E* **44** D3
Piña de Campos *E* **25** D4
Piña de Esgueva *E* **33** A4
Piñar *E* **52** C3
Pinarejo *E* **42** B3
Pineda de Cigüela *E* **42** A3
Pineda de la Sierra *E* **25** D5
Pineda de Mar *E* **37** B5
Pinela *P* **31** B5
Piñel de Abajo *E* **33** B4
Pinhal Novo *P* **38** D2
Pinhanços *P* **30** D3
Pinhão *P* **31** C4
Pinheiro *P* **48** A2
Pinheiro Grande *P* **38** C3
Pinhel *P* **31** C5
Pinilla de Molina *E* **34** D2
Pinilla de Toro *E* **32** B2
Pino *E* **31** B6
Pino del Río *E* **24** C3
Pinofranqueado *E* **31** D6
Piñor *E* **22** D3
Pinoso *E* **54** A3
Pinos-Puente *E* **51** D6
Pinsoro *E* **26** D3
Pintano *E* **27** C4
Pinto *E* **41** A6
Pinzio *P* **31** D5
Piornal *E* **40** A2
Pitarque *E* **35** D5
Pitres *E* **52** D3
Pizarra *E* **57** B5
Placencia de las Armas *E* **26** B2
Plasencia *E* **40** A2
Plasencia del Monte *E* **27** D5
Platja d'Aro *E* **37** A5
Platja de Nules *E* **44** B3
Plentzia *E* **25** B6
Pliego *E* **53** B6
Plou *E* **35** C4
Pobladura del Valle *E* **24** D1
Poblete *E* **41** D5
Poboleda *E* **36** C2
Poceirão *P* **38** D2
Pola de Allande *E* **23** B5
Pola de Laviana *E* **24** B2

Pola de Lena *E* **24** B1
Pola de Siero *E* **24** B2
Pola de Somiedo *E* **23** B6
Polán *E* **41** B5
Poleñino *E* **35** A5
Polientes *E* **25** C4
Pollença *E* **47** B4
Pollensa *E* **47** B4
Pollos *E* **32** B2
Polop *E* **55** A4
Pomaluengo *E* **25** B4
Pomarão *P* **49** C5
Pombal *P* **31** B4
Pombal *P* **38** B3
Pomer *E* **34** B3
Ponferrada *E* **23** C5
Pont de Suert *E* **28** D1
Ponte Aranga *E* **22** B3
Ponteareas *E* **22** D2
Ponte Caldelas *E* **22** D2
Ponteceso *E* **22** B1
Ponte da Barca *P* **30** A2
Ponte de Lima *P* **30** A2
Ponte de Sor *P* **39** C4
Pontedeume *E* **22** B3
Ponte do Rol *P* **38** C1
Ponte Valga *E* **22** C2
Pontevedra *E* **22** D2
Pontével *P* **38** C2
Pontinha *P* **38** D2
Pontones *E* **53** B4
Ponts *E* **36** A2
Pópulo *P* **31** B4
Porcuna *E* **51** B5
Porqueres *E* **29** D5
Porreres *E* **47** C4
Portaje *E* **39** B6
Portalegre *P* **39** C5
Portals Vells *E* **46** C3
Portbou *E* **29** D6
Port d'Andratx *E* **46** B3
Port de Pollença *E* **47** B4
Port de Sóller *E* **46** B3
Portel *P* **49** A4
Portell de Morella *E* **35** D5
Portilla *E* **43** A4
Portilla de la Reina *E* **24** B3
Portillo *E* **32** B3
Portillo de Toledo *E* **41** A5
Portimão *P* **48** D3
Portman *E* **54** C3
Porto *E* **23** D5
Porto *P* **30** C2
Porto Alto *P* **38** D2
Portobravo *E* **22** C2
Porto Colom *E* **47** C4
Porto Covo da Bandeira *P* **48** B2
Porto Cristo *E* **47** B4
Porto de Lagos *P* **48** D3
Porto de Mós *P* **38** B2
Porto do Barqueiro *E* **22** A3
Porto do Son *E* **22** C1
Portomarín *E* **23** C4
Porto Petra *E* **47** C4

Portugalete *E* **25** B6
Porzuna *E* **41** C5
Posada *E* **23** B6
Posada de Valdeón *E* **24** B3
Posadas *E* **51** C4
Potes *E* **24** B3
Pousada *P* **31** D4
Pousos *P* **38** B2
Povedilla *E* **42** D3
Póvoa de Lanhoso *P* **30** B2
Póvoa de São Miguel *P* **49** B5
Póvoa de Varzim *P* **30** B2
Póvoa do Concelho *P* **31** D4
Poyales del Hoyo *E* **40** A3
Poyatos *E* **34** D2
Poza de la Sal *E* **25** C5
Pozaldez *E* **32** B3
Pozo Alcón *E* **53** C4
Pozoamargo *E* **42** C3
Pozoantiguo *E* **32** B2
Pozoblanco *E* **51** A4
Pozo Cañada *E* **43** D4
Pozo de Guadalajara *E* **33** D6
Pozohondo *E* **43** D4
Pozo-Lorente *E* **43** D5
Pozondón *E* **34** D3
Pozorrubio *E* **42** B2
Pozuel del Campo *E* **34** D3
Pozuelo *E* **43** D4
Pozuelo de Alarcón *E* **33** D5
Pozuelo de Aragón *E* **34** B3
Pozuelo del Páramo *E* **24** D1
Pozuelo del Rey *E* **33** D6
Pozuelo de Zarzón *E* **39** A6
Pozuelos de Calatrava *E* **41** D5
Prádanos de Ojeda *E* **25** C4
Pradejón *E* **26** D2
Prádena *E* **33** C5
Pradillo *E* **26** D1
Prado *P* **30** B2
Prado de la Guzpeña *E* **24** C3
Prado del Rey *E* **57** B4
Pradoluengo *E* **25** D6
Praia da Barra *P* **30** D2
Praia da Rocha *P* **48** D3
Praia da Tocha *P* **30** D1
Praia de Esmoriz *P* **30** C2
Praia de Mira *P* **30** D2
Prat de Comte *E* **35** C6
Pratdip *E* **36** C2
Prats de Lluçanès *E* **29** D4
Pravia *E* **23** B6
Premià de Mar *E* **37** B4
Priaranza del Bierzo *E* **23** D5
Priego *E* **34** D2
Priego de Córdoba *E* **51** C5
Prioro *E* **24** C3
Proaza *E* **23** B6
Proba *E* **23** C5
Proença-a-Nova *P* **39** B4
Proença-a-Velha *P* **39** A5

Pruna *E* **51** D4
Puçol *E* **44** B2
Puebla de Albortón *E* **35** B4
Puebla de Alcocer *E* **40** D3
Puebla de Alfindén *E* **35** B4
Puebla de Almenara *E* **42** B2
Puebla de Beleña *E* **33** C6
Puebla de Brollón *E* **23** C4
Puebla de Don Fadrique *E* **53** B5
Puebla de Don Rodrigo *E* **41** C4
Puebla de Guzmán *E* **49** C5
Puebla de la Calzada *E* **39** D6
Puebla de la Reina *E* **40** D2
Puebla de Lillo *E* **24** B2
Puebla del Maestre *E* **50** B2
Puebla del Príncipe *E* **53** A4
Puebla del Prior *E* **50** A2
Puebla del Salvador *E* **43** B4
Puebla de Obando *E* **39** C6
Puebla de Sanabria *E* **31** A5
Puebla de Sancho Pérez *E* **50** A1
Puebla de San Miguel *E* **43** A5
Puebla de San Xulián *E* **23** C4
Puebla de Yeltes *E* **31** D6
Puenteareas *E* **22** D2
Puente de Domingo Flórez *E* **23** D5
Puente de Génave *E* **53** A4
Puente del Congosto *E* **32** D2
Puente de Montañana *E* **28** D1
Puente de San Miguel *E* **25** B4
Puente-Genil *E* **51** C4
Puente la Reina *E* **26** C3
Puentenansa *E* **25** B4
Puente Viesgo *E* **25** B4
Puerto de Béjar *E* **32** D1
Puerto del Son *E* **22** C1
Puerto de Mazarrón *E* **54** C2
Puerto de San Vicente *E* **40** C3
Puerto Lápice *E* **41** C6
Puertollano *E* **41** D5
Puerto Lumbreras *E* **53** C6
Puertomingalvo *E* **43** A6
Puerto Real *E* **56** B3
Puerto Seguro *E* **31** C5
Puerto Serrano *E* **50** D3
Pueyo *E* **26** C3
Pueyo de Santa Cruz *E* **35** A6
Puig *E* **44** B2
Puigcerdà *E* **28** D3
Puigpunyent *E* **46** B3
Puig-reig *E* **36** A3
Pulgar *E* **41** B5
Pulpí *E* **53** C6

Punta Umbría *E* **49** D6
Purchena *E* **53** D5
Purujosa *E* **34** B3
Purullena *E* **52** D3
Puzol *E* **44** B2

Q

Quadrazais *P* **31** D5
Quarteira *P* **49** D4
Quartell *E* **44** B2
Quatretonda *E* **44** D2
Queiriga *P* **30** C3
Quel *E* **26** D2
Queluz *P* **38** D1
Quemada *E* **33** B5
Queralbs *E* **29** D4
Quero *E* **42** C2
Quesa *E* **43** C6
Quesada *E* **52** C3
Quiaios *P* **38** A2
Quintana de la Serena *E* **40** D2
Quintana del Castillo *E* **23** C6
Quintana del Pino *E* **25** C5
Quintana del Puente *E* **25** D4
Quintana de Rueda *E* **24** C2
Quintana-Martín Galíndez *E* **25** C5
Quintanapalla *E* **25** D5
Quintanar de la Orden *E* **42** B2
Quintanar de la Sierra *E* **26** D1
Quintanar del Rey *E* **43** C4
Quintana Redonda *E* **34** B1
Quintanilla de Onésimo *E* **33** B4
Quinto *E* **35** B5
Quintos *P* **49** B4
Quiroga *E* **23** D4
Quiruelas de Vidriales *E* **24** D1
Quismondo *E* **41** A5

R

Rabaçal *P* **31** C4
Rabaçal *P* **38** A3
Rábade *E* **23** B4
Rabanales *E* **31** A6
Rada de Haro *E* **42** B3
Rafelbunyol *E* **44** B2
Rágama *E* **32** C2
Ramales de la Victoria *E* **25** B5
Ramalhal *P* **38** C2
Ramirás *E* **22** D3
Ranhados *P* **30** D3
Raposa *P* **38** C3

Raposeira *P* **48** D2
Rapoula do Côa *P* **31** D5
Rascafría *E* **33** C5
Rasines *E* **25** B5
Rasquera *E* **36** C1
Rasueros *E* **32** C3
Real *P* **30** B3
Rebollosa de Jadraque *E* **33** C6
Rebordelo *E* **22** B3
Rebordelo *P* **31** A4
Recuerda *E* **33** B6
Redinha *P* **38** A3
Redondela *E* **22** D2
Redondelo *P* **31** B4
Redondo *P* **39** D5
Redován *E* **54** B3
Reguengo *E* **22** D2
Reguengos de Monsaraz *P* **49** A5
Reigada *P* **31** C5
Reillo *E* **43** B4
Reina *E* **50** B2
Reinosa *E* **25** B4
Relíquias *P* **48** C3
Relleu *E* **55** A4
Remolinos *E* **35** A4
Rena *E* **40** C2
Renedo *E* **25** B4
Renedo *E* **32** B3
Renedo de la Vega *E* **24** D3
Rentería *E* **26** B2
Requejo *E* **31** A5
Requena *E* **43** C5
Resende *P* **30** C3
Respenda de la Peña *E* **24** C3
Retamal *E* **40** D2
Retortillo *E* **31** C6
Retortillo de Soria *E* **33** B6
Retuerta del Bullaque *E* **41** C5
Reus *E* **36** C2
Revilla de Collazos *E* **24** C3
Revilla del Campo *E* **25** D5
Riachos *P* **38** C3
Rialp *E* **28** D2
Rianjo *E* **22** C2
Riaño *E* **24** B3
Rianxo *E* **22** C2
Riba *E* **25** B5
Ribadavia *E* **22** D3
Ribadelago *E* **23** D5
Riba de Mouro *P* **30** A2
Ribadeo *E* **23** A5
Riba de Saelices *E* **34** C2
Ribadesella *E* **24** A3
Ribaforada *E* **34** A3
Ribafrecha *E* **26** D2
Riba-roja d'Ebre *E* **36** C1
Riba-roja de Turia *E* **43** B6
Ribeira *P* **30** A2
Ribeira de Pena *P* **30** B3
Ribera del Fresno *E* **50** A2
Ribesalbes *E* **44** B2

Ribes de Freser *E* **29** D4
Ribota *E* **33** B5
Ricla *E* **34** B3
Riego de la Vega *E* **23** D6
Riello *E* **23** C6
Rielves *E* **41** B5
Rillo *E* **35** D4
Rillo de Gallo *E* **34** C2
Rincón de la Victoria *E* **57** B6
Rincón de Soto *E* **26** D3
Rio Caldo *P* **30** B3
Rio de Mel *P* **31** C4
Rio de Moinhos *P* **39** D5
Rio de Moinhos *P* **48** B3
Rio de Moinhos *P* **48** B3
Rio de Onor *P* **31** A5
Riofrío *E* **32** D3
Riofrío de Aliste *E* **31** A6
Ríogordo *E* **51** D5
Rioja *E* **53** D5
Riolobos *E* **40** B1
Rio Maior *P* **38** C2
Rionegro del Puente *E* **31** A6
Ríos *E* **31** A4
Rioseco de Tapia *E* **24** C1
Rio Tinto *P* **30** C2
Rio Torto *P* **31** B4
Ripoll *E* **29** D4
Riudarenes *E* **37** A5
Riudecols *E* **36** C2
Riudoms *E* **36** C2
Rivas-Vaciamadrid *E* **33** D5
Rivero *E* **25** B4
Roa *E* **33** B4
Robledo *E* **42** D3
Robledo de Chavela *E* **33** D4
Robledo del Mazo *E* **41** B4
Robledollano *E* **40** B3
Robles de la Valcueva *E* **24** C2
Robliza de Cojos *E* **31** C6
Robregordo *E* **33** C5
Robres *E* **35** A5
Robres del Castillo *E* **26** D2
Rocafort de Queralt *E* **36** B2
Rociana del Condado *E* **49** D6
Roda de Bara *E* **36** C3
Roda de Ter *E* **37** A4
Rodeiro *E* **22** C3
Rodellar *E* **27** D6
Ródenas *E* **34** D3
Rodrigas *E* **23** B4
Rogil *P* **48** C2
Roiz *E* **25** B4
Rojales *E* **54** B3
Rollán *E* **31** C6
Romanones *E* **33** D6
Romeira *P* **38** C2
Romeu *P* **31** B5
Roncal *E* **27** C4
Roncesvalles *E* **26** B3
Ronda *E* **57** B4
Roperuelos del Páramo *E* **24** D1

Roquetas *E* **36** C1
Roquetas de Mar *E* **59** B4
Rosal de la Frontera *E* **49** B5
Rosário *P* **49** C4
Rosell *E* **35** D6
Roses *E* **29** D6
Rosmaninhal *P* **39** B5
Rosselló *E* **36** B1
Rossio ao Sul do Tejo *P* **38** C3
Rota *E* **56** B2
Royuela *E* **34** D3
Rozalén del Monte *E* **42** B2
Ru *E* **22** B3
Rua *P* **31** C4
Rubayo *E* **25** B5
Rubena *E* **25** D5
Rubí *E* **37** B4
Rubiá *E* **23** D5
Rubí de Bracamonte *E* **32** C3
Rubielos de la Cérida *E* **35** D4
Rubielos de Mora *E* **43** A6
Rublacedo de Abajo *E* **25** C5
Rueda *E* **32** B3
Rueda de Jalón *E* **35** B4
Ruente *E* **25** B4
Ruidera *E* **42** D2
Ruivães *P* **30** B3
Rus *E* **52** B3
Rute *E* **51** D5

S

Sabadell *E* **37** B4
Sabero *E* **24** B2
Sabiñánigo *E* **27** C5
Sabiote *E* **52** B3
Sabrosa *P* **31** B4
Sabugal *P* **31** D4
Sabugueiro *P* **31** D4
Sabugueiro *P* **39** D4
Sacañet *E* **43** B6
Sacavém *P* **38** D2
Sacecorbo *E* **34** C2
Sacedón *E* **34** D1
Saceruela *E* **41** D4
Sacramenia *E* **33** B4
Sada *E* **22** B3
Sádaba *E* **27** D4
Saelices *E* **42** B2
Saelices de la Sal *E* **34** C2
Saelices del Rio *E* **24** C3
Saelices de Mayorga *E* **24** D2
Safara *P* **49** B5
Sagres *P* **48** D2
Sagunt *E* **44** B2
Sagunto *E* **44** B2
Sahagún *E* **24** D3
Sahun *E* **27** C6
Salamanca *E* **32** C1
Salar *E* **51** D6
Salardu *E* **28** C2

Salas *E* **23** B6
Salas de los Infantes *E* **25** D5
Saldaña *E* **24** C3
Saldón *E* **43** A5
Salduero *E* **33** A6
Salgueiro *P* **39** B4
Salillas de Jalón *E* **34** B3
Salinas *E* **23** A6
Salinas *E* **54** A3
Salinas de Añana *E* **25** C6
Salinas del Manzano *E* **43** A5
Salinas de Pamplona *E* **26** C3
Salinas de Pisuerga *E* **25** C4
Salir *P* **49** D4
Sallent *E* **36** A3
Sallent de Gállego *E* **27** C5
Salmerón *E* **34** D1
Salmeroncillos de Abajo *E* **34** D1
Salmoral *E* **32** C2
Salobre *E* **53** A4
Salobreña *E* **58** B2
Salorino *E* **39** C5
Salou *E* **36** C2
Salsadella *E* **35** D6
Salt *E* **37** A5
Salteras *E* **50** C2
Salto *P* **30** B3
Salvacañete *E* **43** A5
Salvaleón *E* **49** A6
Salvaterra de Magos *P* **38** D2
Salvaterra do Extremo *P* **39** B6
Salvatierra *E* **26** C2
Salvatierra de los Barros *E* **49** A6
Salvatierra de Santiago *E* **40** C2
Sambade *P* **31** B5
Samboal *E* **33** B4
Sameiro *P* **31** D4
Sames *E* **24** B2
Samil *P* **31** A5
Samir de los Caños *E* **31** B6
Samões *P* **31** B4
Samora Correia *P* **38** D2
Samos *E* **23** C4
Samper de Calanda *E* **35** C5
San Adrián *E* **26** D2
San Agustín de Guadalix *E* **33** D5
San Amaro *E* **22** D3
San Andrés del Rabanedo *E* **24** C2
San Antolín *E* **23** B5
San Antonio *E* **43** C5
San Antonio Abad *E* **45** D5
San Asensio *E* **25** C6
San Bartolomé de las Abiertas *E* **41** B4
San Bartolomé de la Torre *E* **49** C5
San Bartolomé de Pinares *E* **32** D3

San Baudillo de Llobregat *E* 37 B4
San Benito *E* 51 A5
San Benito de la Contienda *E* 39 D5
San Carlos del Valle *E* 42 D2
San Cebrián de Castro *E* 32 B1
Sancellas *E* 47 B4
Sanchidrián *E* 32 C3
San Cibráo das Viñas *E* 22 D3
San Clemente *E* 42 C3
San Clodio *E* 23 D4
San Cosme *E* 23 A4
San Cristóbal de Entreviñas *E* 24 D2
San Cristóbal de la Vega *E* 32 C3
Sancti-Spíritus *E* 31 D6
Sancti-Spíritus *E* 40 D3
Sande *P* 30 C3
Sandiás *E* 22 D3
Sando *E* 31 C6
San Emiliano *E* 23 C6
San Esteban de Gormaz *E* 33 B6
San Esteban de la Sierra *E* 32 D1
San Esteban de Litera *E* 35 A6
San Esteban del Molar *E* 32 A2
San Esteban del Valle *E* 41 A4
San Felices de los Gallegos *E* 31 C5
San Fernando *E* 56 B2
San Fernando de Henares *E* 33 D5
Sanfins do Douro *P* 31 B4
San Francisco Javier *E* 45 D6
Sangarcía *E* 33 C4
Sangenjo *E* 22 D2
Sangüesa *E* 27 C4
San Guim de Freixenet *E* 36 B3
San Ildefonso *E* 33 C4
San Javier *E* 54 C3
San Jorge *E* 35 D6
San Jorge de Alor *E* 39 D5
San José *E* 45 D5
San José *E* 59 B5
San José del Valle *E* 56 B3
San José de Malcocinado *E* 56 C3
San Juan Bautista *E* 45 C6
San Juan de Alicante *E* 55 A4
San Juan de Aznalfarache *E* 50 C2
San Juan de la Nava *E* 32 D3
San Juan del Puerto *E* 49 D6
San Justo de la Vega *E* 23 D6
San Leonardo de Yagüe *E* 33 A6

San Lorenzo de Calatrava *E* 51 A6
San Lorenzo de El Escorial *E* 33 D4
San Lorenzo de la Parrilla *E* 42 B3
Sanlúcar de Barrameda *E* 56 B2
Sanlúcar de Guadiana *E* 49 C5
Sanlúcar la Mayor *E* 50 C2
San Luis *E* 47 B6
San Mamés de Campos *E* 24 D3
San Marcos *E* 22 B2
San Martín *E* 25 B4
San Martín *E* 26 B2
San Martín de la Vega *E* 41 A6
San Martín de la Vega del Alberche *E* 32 D2
San Martin del Pimpollar *E* 32 D3
San Martín de Montalbán *E* 41 B5
San Martín de Pusa *E* 41 B4
San Martín de Unx *E* 26 C3
San Martín de Valdeiglesias *E* 33 D4
San Mateo de Gállego *E* 35 A4
San Miguel de Arroyo *E* 33 B4
San Miguel de Bernuy *E* 33 B4
San Miguel de Salinas *E* 54 B3
San Millán de la Cogolla *E* 25 D6
San Nicolás del Puerto *E* 50 B3
San Pablo de los Montes *E* 41 B5
San Pedro *E* 42 D3
San Pedro de Alcántara *E* 57 B5
San Pedro de Ceque *E* 24 D1
San Pedro del Arroyo *E* 32 C3
San Pedro de Latarce *E* 32 B2
San Pedro del Pinatar *E* 54 C3
San Pedro del Romeral *E* 25 B5
San Pedro de Rozados *E* 32 C1
San Pedro Manrique *E* 26 D2
San Pedro Palmiches *E* 34 D2
San Rafael del Río *E* 35 D6
San Román *E* 23 C5
San Román de Cameros *E* 26 D2
San Román de la Cuba *E* 24 D3

San Román de los Montes *E* 41 A4
San Roque *E* 22 B2
San Roque *E* 22 D3
San Roque *E* 57 C4
San Salvador de Cantamunda *E* 24 C3
San Sebastián de los Ballesteros *E* 51 C4
San Sebastián de los Reyes *E* 33 D5
San Silvestre de Guzmán *E* 49 C5
Sansol *E* 26 C2
Santa Amalia *E* 40 D2
Santa Ana *E* 43 D4
Santa Ana de Pusa *E* 41 B4
Santa Ana la Real *E* 49 B6
Santa Bàrbara *E* 36 D1
Santa Bárbara de Casa *E* 49 C5
Santacara *E* 26 D3
Santa Cataliña de Armada *E* 22 B2
Santa Catarina *P* 48 A3
Santa Catarina da Fonte do Bispo *P* 49 D4
Santa Cilia de Jaca *E* 27 C4
Santa Clara-a-Nova *P* 49 C4
Santa Clara-a-Velha *P* 48 C3
Santa Clara de Louredo *P* 49 B4
Santa Coloma de Farners *E* 37 A5
Santa Coloma de Queralt *E* 36 B3
Santa Colomba de Somoza *E* 23 D6
Santa Columba de Curueño *E* 24 C2
Santa Comba Dão *P* 30 D3
Santa Comba de Rossas *P* 31 B5
Santa Cristina d'Aro *E* 37 A5
Santa Cristina de la Polvorosa *E* 32 A1
Santa Cruz *P* 48 B2
Santa Cruz da Tapa *P* 30 C3
Santa Cruz de Bezana *E* 25 B4
Santa Cruz de la Serós *E* 27 C5
Santa Cruz de la Sierra *E* 40 C2
Santa Cruz de la Zarza *E* 42 B2
Santa Cruz de los Cáñamos *E* 42 D2
Santa Cruz del Retamar *E* 41 A5
Santa Cruz de Moya *E* 43 B5
Santa Cruz de Mudela *E* 41 D6
Santa Elena *E* 52 A3
Santa Elena de Jamuz *E* 23 D6

Santaella *E* 51 C4
Santa Engracia *E* 26 D2
Santa Eufemia *E* 41 D4
Santa Eugèni *E* 47 B4
Santa Eulalia *E* 23 B6
Santa Eulalia *E* 24 B2
Santa Eulalia *E* 34 D3
Santa Eulalia *P* 39 D5
Santa Eulalia del Río *E* 45 D6
Santa Eulalia de Oscos *E* 23 B5
Santa Eulàlia de Riuprimer *E* 37 A4
Santa Fé *E* 51 D6
Sant Agustí de Lluçanès *E* 29 D4
Santa Iria *P* 49 B5
Santa Justa *P* 38 D3
Santa Kurutze Kanpezu *E* 26 C2
Santalha *P* 31 A4
Santa Liestra y San Quílez *E* 27 D6
Santa Lucía de Moraña *E* 22 C2
Santa Luzia *P* 48 C3
Santa Magdalena de Pulpís *E* 35 D6
Santa Margarida da Serra *P* 48 B3
Santa Margarida de Montbui *E* 36 B3
Santa Margarida do Sádão *P* 48 B3
Santa Margarita *E* 47 B4
Santa María *E* 27 D4
Santa María da Feira *P* 30 C2
Santa María de Cayón *E* 25 B5
Santa María de Corcó *E* 29 D4
Santa María de Huertas *E* 34 C2
Santa Maria del Berrocal *E* 32 D2
Santa María del Camino *E* 46 B3
Santa María del Campo *E* 25 D4
Santa María del Campo Rus *E* 42 B3
Santa María de los Llanos *E* 42 C2
Santa María del Páramo *E* 24 D1
Santa María del Val *E* 34 D2
Santa María de Nieva *E* 53 C5
Santa María de Palautordera *E* 37 B4
Santa María la Real de Nieva *E* 33 C4
Santa Marina del Rey *E* 24 C1

Santa Marta *E* **39** D6
Santa Marta *E* **42** C3
Santa Marta de Penaguião *P* **30** C3
Santa Marta de Tormes *E* **32** C2
Santana *P* **38** A2
Santana *P* **48** A2
Santana da Serra *P* **48** C3
Santana de Cambas *P* **49** C5
Santana do Mato *P* **38** D3
Santander *E* **25** A5
Santanyí *E* **47** C4
Santa Olalla *E* **41** A5
Santa Oliva *E* **36** C3
Santa Ollala del Cala *E* **50** B2
Santa Pau *E* **29** D5
Santa Pola *E* **55** B4
Santar *P* **30** D3
Santarém *P* **38** C3
Santas Martas *E* **24** D2
Santa Sofia *P* **39** D4
Santa Susana *P* **48** A3
Santa Susana *P* **49** A4
Santa Uxía de Ribeira *E* **22** C1
Santa Vitória *P* **49** B4
Santa Vitória do Ameixial *P* **39** D4
Sant Boi de Llobregat *E* **37** B4
Sant Carles de la Ràpita *E* **36** D1
Sant Celoni *E* **37** B4
Sant Cugat del Vallès *E* **37** B4
San Telmo *E* **49** C6
Santervás de la Vega *E* **24** C3
Santes Creus *E* **36** B2
Sant Feliu de Guíxols *E* **37** A5
Sant Feliu de Pallerols *E* **29** D4
Sant Feliu Sasserra *E* **37** A4
Sant Hilari Sacalm *E* **37** A4
Sant Hipòlit de Voltregà *E* **29** D4
Santiago de Alcántara *E* **39** B5
Santiago de Calatrava *E* **51** C5
Santiago de Compostela *E* **22** C2
Santiago de Covelo *E* **22** D2
Santiago de la Espada *E* **53** B4
Santiago de la Ribera *E* **54** C3
Santiago del Campo *E* **40** B1
Santiago do Cacém *P* **48** B2
Santiago do Escoural *P* **48** A3
Santiagomillas *E* **23** D6
Santibáñez de Béjar *E* **32** D2

Santibáñez de la Peña *E* **24** C3
Santibáñez de la Sierra *E* **32** D1
Santibáñez de Tera *E* **31** A6
Santibáñez de Vidriales *E* **24** D1
Santibáñez el Bajo *E* **40** A1
Santibáñez Zarzaguda *E* **25** D5
Santillana *E* **25** B4
Santiponce *E* **50** C2
Santisteban del Puerto *E* **52** B3
Santiuste de San Juan Bautista *E* **32** C3
Santiz *E* **32** C1
Sant Jaume del Mediterrani *E* **47** B6
Sant Jaume d'Enveja *E* **36** D1
Sant Joan de les Abadesses *E* **29** D4
Sant Joan de Vilatorrada *E* **36** B3
Sant Joan les Fonts *E* **29** D4
Sant Julià de Lòria *AND* **28** D3
Sant Llorenç de Morunys *E* **28** D3
Sant Llorenç des Cardassar *E* **47** B4
Sant Martí de Tous *E* **36** B3
Sant Martí Sarroca *E* **36** B3
Sant Mateu *E* **35** D6
Sant Miquel *E* **45** D6
Santo Aleixo *P* **39** D5
Santo Aleixo da Restauração *P* **49** B5
Santo Amador *P* **49** B5
Santo André *P* **48** B2
Santo Antoninho *E* **22** D2
Santo António dos Cavaleiros *P* **38** D2
Santo Domingo de la Calzada *E* **25** D6
Santo Domingo de Silos *E* **33** A5
Santo Estêvão *P* **38** D2
Santo Estêvão *P* **49** D4
Santo Isidro de Pegões *P* **38** D3
Santomera *E* **54** B3
Santoña *E* **25** B5
Santo Tirso *P* **30** B2
Santo Tomé *E* **52** B3
Santovenia *E* **32** A1
Santpedor *E* **36** A3
Sant Pere de Ribes *E* **36** C3
Sant Pere de Torelló *E* **29** D4
Sant Pere Pescador *E* **29** D5
Sant Pol de Mar *E* **37** B5
Sant Privat d'en Bas *E* **29** D4
Sant Quintí de Mediona *E* **36** B3

Sant Quirze de Besora *E* **29** D4
Sant Sadurní d'Anoia *E* **36** B3
Sant Telm *E* **46** B3
Santullano *E* **23** B6
Santurce *E* **25** B6
Santurtzi *E* **25** B6
Sant Vicenç dels Horts *E* **37** B4
Sant Vicent del Raspeig *E* **55** A4
Sant Vincenç de Castellet *E* **36** B3
San Vicente de Alcántara *E* **39** C5
San Vicente de la Barquera *E* **25** B4
San Vicente de la Sonsierra *E* **25** C6
San Vicente del Raspeig *E* **55** A4
San Vicente de Palacio *E* **32** C3
San Vicente de Toranzo *E* **25** B4
San Vicenzo *E* **22** C2
San Vitero *E* **31** A6
Sanxenxo *E* **22** D2
Sanzoles *E* **32** B2
São Barnabé *P* **48** C3
São Bartolomeu *P* **39** C4
São Bartolomeu da Serra *P* **48** B3
São Bartolomeu de Messines *P* **48** D3
São Bento do Cortiço *P* **39** D5
São Brás *P* **49** B4
São Brás de Alportel *P* **49** D4
São Brás do Regedouro *P* **49** A4
São Brissos *P* **49** B4
São Cosmado *P* **31** C4
São Domingos *P* **48** B3
São Facundo *P* **39** C4
São Francisco da Serra *P* **48** B3
São Geraldo *P* **38** D3
São Gregório *P* **39** D4
São Jacinto *P* **30** D2
São João da Madeira *P* **30** C2
São João da Pesqueira *P* **31** C4
São João da Venda *P* **49** D4
São João do Campo *P* **38** A3
São João dos Caldeireiros *P* **49** C4
São José da Lamarosa *P* **38** C3
São Lourenço de Mamporcão *P* **39** D5
São Luís *P* **48** C3
São Manços *P* **49** A4
São Marcos da Ataboeira *P* **49** C4

São Marcos da Serra *P* **48** C3
São Marcos do Campo *P* **49** A5
São Martinho da Cortiça *P* **38** A3
São Martinho das Amoreiras *P* **48** C3
São Martinho de Angueira *P* **31** B6
São Martinho do Porto *P* **38** B2
São Matias *P* **49** B4
São Miguel de Acha *P* **39** A5
São Miguel de Machede *P* **39** D4
São Miguel de Rio Torto *P* **38** C3
São Miguel do Outeiro *P* **30** D3
São Miguel do Pinheiro *P* **49** C4
São Pedro da Cadeira *P* **38** C1
São Pedro de Muel *P* **38** B2
São Pedro de Solis *P* **49** C4
São Pedro do Sul *P* **30** D3
São Romão *P* **39** D5
São Romão do Sado *P* **48** B3
São Sebastião dos Carros *P* **49** C4
São Teotónio *P* **48** C2
São Vicente *P* **31** A4
São Vicente da Beira *P* **39** A5
Sa Pobla *E* **47** B4
Sa Ràpita *E* **47** C4
Sardoal *P* **38** B3
S'Arenal *E* **46** C3
Sariegos *E* **24** C2
Sariñena *E* **35** A5
Sarnadas do Ródão *P* **39** B4
Sarracín *E* **25** D5
Sarral *E* **36** B2
Sarraquinhos *P* **30** A3
Sarreaus *E* **23** D4
Sarria *E* **23** C4
Sarrià de Ter *E* **29** D5
Sarrión *E* **43** A6
Sarroca de Lleida *E* **36** B1
Sartaguda *E* **26** D2
Sarvisé *E* **27** C5
Sarzedas *P* **39** B4
Sarzedo *P* **31** C4
Sasamón *E* **25** D4
Sástago *E* **35** B5
Satão *P* **30** D3
Saúca *E* **34** C1
Sax *E* **54** A3
Sayalonga *E* **57** B6
Sayatón *E* **33** D6
Seara *P* **30** A2
Sebal *P* **38** A3
Sedano *E* **25** C5
Segorbe *E* **43** B6
Segovia *E* **33** C4

Segura *P* **39** B6
Segura de la Sierra *E* **53** B4
Segura de León *E* **49** B6
Segura de los Baños *E* **35** C4
Segurilla *E* **41** A4
Seia *P* **30** D3
Seixal *P* **38** D2
Selaya *E* **25** B5
Sella *E* **55** A4
Selmes *P* **49** B4
Selva *E* **47** B4
Semide *P* **38** A3
Sena *E* **35** B6
Sendim *P* **30** B3
Sendim *P* **31** B6
Senes *E* **53** D5
Senhora do Rosário *P* **39** C5
Senterada *E* **28** D2
Seo de Urgell *E* **28** D3
Sepulcro-Hilario *E* **31** D6
Sepúlveda *E* **33** B5
Sequeros *E* **31** D6
Serinyà *E* **29** D5
Sernancelhe *P* **31** C4
Serón *E* **53** D4
Serón de Nájima *E* **34** B2
Seròs *E* **35** B6
Serpa *E* **49** B5
Serpins *P* **38** A3
Serra *E* **44** B2
Serrada *E* **32** B3
Serradilla *E* **40** B2
Serradilla del Arroyo *E* **31** D6
Serranillos *E* **32** D3
Serrejón *E* **40** B2
Sertã *P* **39** B4
Serzedo *P* **30** C2
Sesa *E* **35** A5
Seseña *E* **41** A6
Sesma *E* **26** C2
Ses Salines *E* **47** C4
Sestao *E* **25** B6
Setenil *E* **57** B4
Setiles *E* **34** D3
Setúbal *P* **48** A2
Seva *E* **37** A4
Sever do Vouga *P* **30** D2
Sevilla *E* **50** C2
Sevilla la Nueva *E* **33** D4
Sevilleja de la Jara *E* **41** B4
Sierra de Fuentes *E* **40** C1
Sierra de Luna *E* **27** D4
Sierra de Yeguas *E* **51** D4
Sierra Engarcerán *E* **44** A3
Sierro *E* **53** D5
Siete Iglesias de Trabancos *E* **32** B2
Sigüeiro *E* **22** C2
Sigüenza *E* **34** C1
Sigües *E* **27** C4
Siles *E* **53** A4
Silla *E* **44** C2
Silleda *E* **22** C3
Sils *E* **37** A5
Silvares *P* **39** A4

Silveiras *P* **38** D3
Simancas *E* **32** B3
Simat de la Valdigna *E* **44** D2
Sinarcas *E* **43** B5
Sines *P* **48** B2
Sineu *E* **47** B4
Sinlabajos *E* **32** C3
Sintra *P* **38** D1
Siruela *E* **41** D4
Sisante *E* **42** C3
Sitges *E* **36** C3
Soajo *P* **30** A3
Sobradelo *E* **23** D5
Sobradiel *E* **35** B4
Sobrado *E* **22** B3
Sobrado *E* **22** D3
Sobral da Adiça *P* **49** B5
Sobral de Monte Agraço *P* **38** D2
Sobreira Formosa *P* **39** B4
Socovos *E* **53** A5
Socuéllamos *E* **42** C2
Solana de los Barros *E* **39** D6
Solana del Pino *E* **51** A6
Solana de Rioalmar *E* **32** D3
Soldeu *AND* **28** C3
Solivella *E* **36** B2
Sóller *E* **46** B3
Solórzano *E* **25** B5
Solosancho *E* **32** D3
Solsona *E* **36** A3
Somontín *E* **53** C5
Soncillo *E* **25** C5
Soneja *E* **44** B2
Sonim *P* **31** B4
Sonseca *E* **41** B5
Son Servera *E* **47** B5
Sopeira *E* **28** D1
Sopelana *E* **25** B6
Sorbas *E* **53** D5
Soria *E* **34** A2
Sorihuela *E* **32** D1
Sorihuela del Gaudalimar *E* **52** B3
Sort *E* **28** D2
Sortelha *P* **31** D4
Sorvilán *E* **58** B3
Sos del Rey Católico *E* **27** C4
Soses *E* **35** B6
Sotés *E* **26** D1
Sotiel Coronada *E* **49** C6
Sotillo de la Adrada *E* **41** A4
Sotillo del Rincón *E* **34** A1
Soto *E* **23** A6
Soto de la Vega *E* **23** D6
Soto del Real *E* **33** D5
Soto de Ribera *E* **23** B6
Soto en Cameros *E* **26** D2
Sotopalacios *E* **25** D5
Sotos *E* **42** A3
Sotoserrano *E* **31** D6
Soto y Amio *E* **23** C6
Sotres *P* **24** B3
Sotresgudo *E* **25** C4

Sotrondio *E* **24** B2
Sotuélamos *E* **42** D3
Soure *P* **38** A3
Souro Pires *P* **31** D4
Sousel *P* **39** D4
Souto *E* **22** C3
Souto *P* **30** B2
Souto *P* **31** D5
Souto *P* **38** B3
Souto da Casa *P* **39** A5
Suances *E* **25** B4
Sucina *E* **54** B3
Sudanell *E* **36** B1
Sueca *E* **44** C2
Sunbilla *E* **26** B3
Súria *E* **36** A3

T

Tabanera de Cerrato *E* **25** D4
Tábara *E* **31** A6
Tabernas *E* **53** D5
Taberno *E* **53** C5
Taboada *E* **22** C3
Taboadela *E* **22** D3
Tábua *P* **30** D3
Tabuaço *P* **31** C4
Tabuenca *E* **34** B3
Tafalla *E* **26** C3
Tahal *E* **53** D5
Taíde *P* **30** B3
Talamantes *E* **34** B3
Talarrubias *E* **40** D3
Talaván *E* **40** B1
Talavera de la Reina *E* **41** B4
Talavera la Real *E* **39** D6
Talayuela *E* **40** B3
Talayuelas *E* **43** B5
Tales *E* **44** B2
Talhadas *P* **30** D2
Táliga *E* **49** A6
Tallós *E* **22** C2
Tama *E* **24** B3
Tamajón *E* **33** C6
Tamames *E* **31** D6
Tamarite de Litera *E* **35** A6
Tamurejo *E* **41** D4
Tapia de Casariego *E* **23** A5
Taracena *E* **33** D6
Taradell *E* **37** A4
Taramundi *E* **23** B4
Tarancón *E* **42** B2
Tarazona *E* **34** A3
Tarazona de la Mancha *E* **43** C4
Tárbena *E* **44** D3
Tardajos *E* **25** D5
Tardelcuende *E* **34** B1
Tardienta *E* **35** A5
Tarifa *E* **57** C4
Tarouca *P* **30** C3
Tarragona *E* **36** C2
Tarrasa *E* **37** B4
Tàrrega *E* **36** B2

Tarrio *E* **22** B2
Tarroja de Segarra *E* **36** B2
Tauste *E* **35** A4
Taveiro *P* **38** A3
Tavernes de la Valldigna *E* **44** D2
Tavertet *E* **37** A4
Tavira *P* **49** D4
Tazones *E* **24** A2
Teba *E* **51** D4
Tebar *E* **42** C3
Teixeiro *E* **22** B3
Teixoso *P* **31** D4
Tejadillos *E* **43** A4
Tejado *E* **34** B2
Tejeda de Tiétar *E* **40** A2
Telhado *P* **39** A5
Telões *P* **30** B3
Tembleque *E* **41** B6
Tendilla *E* **33** D6
Tentúgal *P* **38** A3
Terena *P* **39** D5
Teresa *E* **43** B6
Teresa de Cofrentes *E* **43** C5
Térmens *E* **36** B1
Terrades *E* **29** D5
Terrassa *E* **37** B4
Terriente *E* **43** A5
Terrinches *E* **42** D2
Terrugem *P* **38** D1
Terrugem *P* **39** D5
Teruel *E* **35** D4
Teulada *E* **44** D3
Tharsis *E* **49** C5
Tibi *E* **55** A4
Tiebas *E* **26** C3
Tiedra *E* **32** B2
Tierga *E* **34** B3
Tierzo *E* **34** D2
Tíjola *E* **53** D5
Tinajas *E* **34** D1
Tinalhas *P* **39** B5
Tineo *E* **23** B6
Tiñosillos *E* **32** C3
Tirgo *E* **25** C6
Tiriez *E* **42** D3
Tirig *E* **35** D6
Tirteafuera *E* **41** D5
Titaguas *E* **43** B5
Titulcia *E* **41** A6
Tivenys *E* **36** C1
Tivissa *E* **36** C1
Tobarra *E* **53** A6
Tocha *P* **30** D2
Tocón *E* **51** D6
Todolella *E* **35** D5
Toén *E* **22** D3
Tolbaños *E* **32** D3
Toledo *E* **41** B5
Tolosa *E* **26** B2
Tolosa *P* **39** C4
Tolox *E* **57** B5
Tolva *E* **28** D1
Tomar *P* **38** B3
Tomares *E* **50** C2

Tomelloso E 42 C2
Tona E 37 A4
Tondela P 30 D3
Topares E 53 B5
Torá E 36 A3
Toral de los Guzmanes E 24 D2
Toral de los Vados E 23 C5
Tordehumos E 32 A2
Tordera E 37 B5
Tordesillas E 32 B3
Tordesilos E 34 D3
Torellano E 55 B4
Torelló E 29 D4
Toreno E 23 C5
Torija E 33 D6
Torla E 27 C5
Tormón E 43 A5
Tornadizos de Ávila E 32 D3
Tornavacas E 40 A2
Tornos E 34 C3
Toro E 32 B2
Torquemada E 25 D4
Torraiba de Calatrava E 41 D6
Torralba E 42 A3
Torralba de Aragón E 35 A5
Torralba de El Burgo E 33 B6
Torralba de Oropesa E 40 B3
Torralba de Sisones E 34 C3
Torrão P 48 A3
Torre-Alháquime E 51 D4
Torrebaja E 43 A5
Torreblanca E 44 A3
Torreblascopedro E 51 B6
Torrecaballeros E 33 C4
Torrecampo E 51 A5
Torre-Cardela E 52 C3
Torrecilla de Alcañiz E 35 C6
Torrecilla de la Jara E 41 B4
Torrecilla de la Orden E 32 C2
Torrecilla del Rebollar E 35 C4
Torrecillas de la Tiesa E 40 B2
Torre da Gadanha P 48 A3
Torre das Vargens P 39 C4
Torre de Coelheiros P 49 A4
Torre de Dona Chama P 31 B4
Torre de Embesora E 35 D6
Torredeita P 30 D3
Torre de Juan Abad E 52 A3
Torre del Bierzo E 23 C6
Torre del Burgo E 33 C6
Torre del Campo E 51 C6
Torre del Mar E 57 B6
Torredembarra E 36 C3
Torre de Miguel Sesmero E 39 D6
Torre de Moncorvo P 31 C5
Torre de Santa María E 40 C2

Torredonjimeno E 51 C6
Torre do Terrenho P 31 C4
Torrefarrera E 36 B1
Torregamones E 31 B6
Torregrossa E 36 B2
Torreiglesias E 33 C4
Torreira P 30 D2
Torrejoncillo E 39 B6
Torrejoncillo del Rey E 42 B3
Torrejón de Ardoz E 33 D5
Torrejón del Rey E 33 D6
Torrejón el Rubio E 40 B2
Torrelacarcel E 34 D3
Torrelaguna E 33 C5
Torrelapaja E 34 B2
Torrelavega E 25 B4
Torrellas E 34 A3
Torrelles de Foix E 36 B3
Torrelobatón E 32 B3
Torrelodones E 33 D4
Torremanzanas - La Torre de les Macanes E 55 A4
Torremayor E 39 D6
Torremegía E 40 D1
Torremocha E 40 C2
Torremocha de Jiloca E 34 D3
Torremolinos E 57 B6
Torrenostra E 44 A3
Torrent E 44 C2
Torrente E 44 C2
Torrente del Cinca E 35 B6
Torrenueva E 42 D1
Torreorgaz E 40 C1
Torre-Pacheco E 54 C3
Torreperogil E 52 B3
Torres E 52 C3
Torresandino E 33 A5
Torres de Albánchez E 53 A4
Torres de Berrellén E 35 B4
Torres de la Alameda E 33 D5
Torres del Carrizal E 32 B1
Torresmenudas E 32 C1
Torres Novas P 38 C3
Torres Vedras P 38 C1
Torrevelilla E 35 C6
Torrevieja E 54 B3
Torrico E 40 B3
Torrijas E 43 A6
Torrijo E 34 B3
Torrijo del Campo E 34 C3
Torrijos E 41 B5
Torroal P 48 A2
Torroella de Montgrí E 29 D5
Torrox E 58 B2
Torrubia del Campo E 42 B2
Torrubia de Soria E 34 B2
Tortellà E 29 D5
Tórtola de Henares E 33 D6
Tórtoles de Esgueva E 33 A4
Tortosa E 36 C1
Tortozendo P 39 A5
Tortuera E 34 C3
Torvizcón E 58 A3

Tossa E 37 B5
Totana E 53 C6
Touça P 31 C4
Tous E 43 C6
Trabada E 23 B4
Trabanca E 31 C6
Trabazos E 31 A5
Tragacete E 34 D3
Traid E 34 D3
Traiguera E 35 D6
Tramacastilla E 34 D3
Tramagal P 38 C3
Trancoso P 31 C4
Trasmiras E 31 A4
Trasobares E 34 B3
Travanca do Mondego P 30 D3
Travassô P 30 D2
Trebolle E 23 C4
Trebujena E 56 A3
Tremedal de Tormes E 31 C6
Tremês P 38 C2
Tremp E 28 D2
Tresjuncos E 42 B2
Trespaderne E 25 C5
Trevélez E 52 D3
Treviana E 25 C6
Treviño E 25 C6
Trevões P 31 C4
Triacastela E 23 C4
Trigaches P 49 B4
Trigueros E 49 C6
Trigueros del Valle E 32 A3
Trillo E 34 C3
Trindade P 31 B4
Trindade P 49 B4
Trinta P 31 D4
Triollo E 24 C3
Trofa P 30 B2
Tróia P 48 A2
Tronco P 31 A4
Troviscal P 39 B4
Trubia E 23 B6
Truchas E 23 D6
Trujillanos E 40 D1
Trujillo E 40 C2
Tubilla del Agua E 25 C5
Tudela E 26 D3
Tudela de Duero E 32 B3
Tuejar E 43 B5
Tui E 30 A2
Turcia E 23 C6
Turcifal P 38 C1
Turégano E 33 C4
Turís E 43 C6
Turleque E 41 B6
Turquel P 38 C2
Turre E 53 D6
Tutera E 26 D3
Túy E 30 A2

U

Úbeda E 52 B3

Ubidea E 25 B6
Ubrique E 57 B4
Uceda E 33 C5
Ucero E 33 B6
Ucha P 30 B2
Uclés E 42 B2
Ugarana E 25 B6
Ugíjar E 52 D3
Uharte-Arakil E 26 C2
Uleila del Campo E 53 D5
Ulldecona E 35 D6
Ulldemolins E 36 B2
Ulme E 38 C3
Uña E 43 A4
Uña de Quintana E 23 D6
Uncastillo E 27 D4
Unhais da Serra P 39 A4
Unhais-o-Velho P 39 A4
Urda E 41 C6
Urdax-Urdazuli E 26 B3
Urnieta E 26 B2
Urrea de Gaén E 35 C5
Urrea de Jalón E 35 B4
Urretxu E 26 B2
Urriés E 27 C4
Urros P 31 C5
Urroz E 26 C3
Urueña E 32 B2
Usagre E 50 A2
Usurbil E 26 B2
Utebo E 35 B4
Utiel E 43 B5
Utrera E 50 D3
Utrillas E 35 D4

V

Vadocondes E 33 B5
Vagos P 30 D2
Vaiamonte P 39 C5
Valada P 38 C2
Valadares P 22 D2
Valareña E 26 D3
Valbom P 30 C2
Valbona E 43 A6
Valbuena de Duero E 33 B4
Valdealgorfa E 35 C6
Valdecaballeros E 40 C3
Valdecañas de Tajo E 40 B3
Valdecarros E 32 D2
Valdecilla E 25 B5
Valdecuenca E 43 A5
Valdefuentes E 40 C2
Valdeganga E 43 C4
Valdelacasa E 32 D1
Valdelacasa de Tajo E 40 B3
Valdelamusa E 49 C6
Valdelinares E 35 D5
Valdemanco del Esteras E 41 D4
Valdemeca E 43 A4
Valdemorillo E 33 D4
Valdemoro E 41 A6
Valdemoro-Sierra E 43 A4

Valdenoches *E* **33** D6
Valdeobispo *E* **40** A1
Valdeolivas *E* **34** D2
Valdepeñas *E* **41** D6
Valdepeñas de Jaén *E* **51** C6
Valderas *E* **24** D2
Valderrobes *E* **35** C6
Val de Santo Domingo *E*
41 A5
Valdestillas *E* **32** B3
Valdetormo *E* **35** C6
Valdetorres *E* **40** D2
Valdeverdeja *E* **40** B3
Valdevimbre *E* **24** D2
Valdilecha *E* **42** A1
Valdunquillo *E* **24** D2
Vale da Rosa *P* **49** D4
Vale das Mós *P* **39** C4
Vale de Açor *P* **39** C4
Vale de Açor *P* **49** C4
Vale de Cambra *P* **30** C2
Vale de Cavalos *P* **38** C3
Vale de Espinho *P* **31** D5
Vale de Estrela *P* **31** D4
Vale de Figueira *P* **38** C3
Vale de Lobo *P* **49** D4
Vale de Prazeres *P* **39** A5
Vale de Reis *P* **48** A3
Vale de Salgueiro *P* **31** B4
Vale de Santarém *P* **38** C2
Vale do Peso *P* **39** C4
Válega *P* **30** C2
Valença *P* **30** A2
Valença do Douro *P* **31** C4
Valencia *E* **44** C2
Valencia de Alcántara *E*
39 C5
Valencia de Don Juan *E*
24 D2
Valencia de las Torres *E*
50 A2
Valencia del Mombuey *E*
49 B5
Valencia del Ventoso *E* **49** A6
Valenzuela *E* **51** C5
Valenzuela de Calatrava *E*
41 D6
Valera de Arriba *E* **43** B4
Vales Mortos *P* **49** C5
Valfarta *E* **35** B5
Valhelhas *P* **31** D4
Valhermoso *E* **34** D2
Valjunquera *E* **35** C6
Valladolid *E* **32** B3
Valladolises *E* **54** C3
Vallbona d'Anoia *E* **36** B3
Vall d'Alba *E* **44** A3
Valldemossa *E* **46** B3
Vall de Uxó *E* **44** B3
Valle *E* **25** B4
Valle de Abdalajís *E* **51** D5
Valle de la Serena *E* **40** D2
Valle de Matamoros *E* **49** A6
Valle de Santa Ana *E* **49** A6
Vallenca *E* **43** A5

Vallfogona de Riucorb *E*
36 B2
Vallmoll *E* **36** C2
Valls *E* **36** B2
Valmadrid *E* **35** B4
Valmojado *E* **41** A5
Valongo *P* **30** C2
Valongo *P* **39** C4
Válor *E* **52** D3
Valoria la Buena *E* **32** A3
Valpaços *P* **31** B4
Valpalmas *E* **27** D4
Valseca *E* **33** C4
Valsequillo *E* **50** A3
Valtablado del Río *E* **34** D2
Valtiendas *E* **33** B4
Valtierra *E* **26** D3
Valverde de Burguillos *E*
49 A6
Valverde de Júcar *E* **42** B3
Valverde de la Virgen *E*
24 C1
Valverde del Camino *E*
49 C6
Valverde de Leganés *E*
39 D6
Valverde del Fresno *E* **39** A6
Valverde de Llerena *E* **50** B2
Valverde del Majano *E* **33** C4
Valverde de Mérida *E* **40** D1
Vandellós *E* **36** C2
Vañes *E* **24** C3
Vaqueiros *P* **49** C4
Vara del Rey *E* **42** C3
Vecinos *E* **32** C1
Vedra *E* **22** C2
Vegacervera *E* **24** C2
Vega de Espinareda *E* **23** C5
Vegadeo *E* **23** B5
Vega de Pas *E* **25** B5
Vega de Tirados *E* **32** C1
Vega de Valcarce *E* **23** C5
Vega de Valdetronco *E* **32** B2
Veganzones *E* **33** C4
Vegaquemada *E* **24** C2
Vegarienza *E* **23** C6
Vegas del Condado *E* **24** C2
Vegas de Matute *E* **33** C4
Veiros *P* **39** D5
Vejer de la Frontera *E* **56** C3
Velamazán *E* **34** B1
Velefique *E* **53** D5
Vélez-Blanco *E* **53** C5
Vélez de Benaudalla *E* **58** B3
Vélez-Málaga *E* **57** B6
Vélez-Rubio *E* **53** C5
Velilla de Cinca *E* **35** B6
Velilla del Río Carrión *E*
24 C3
Vellisca *E* **42** A2
Venda Nova *P* **30** B3
Vendas Novas *P* **38** D3
Vendinha *P* **49** A4
Venialbo *E* **32** B2
Venta de Baños *E* **32** A3

Venta del Charco *E* **51** B5
Venta del Moro *E* **43** C5
Venta de los Santos *E* **52** A3
Venta las Ranas *E* **24** A2
Venta Nueva *E* **23** B5
Ventas de Huelma *E* **51** D6
Ventas de Zafarraya *E* **51** D6
Vera *E* **53** D6
Vera Cruz *P* **49** B4
Vergara *E* **26** B2
Verges *E* **29** D5
Verín *E* **31** A4
Vermiosa *E* **31** C5
Vermoil *P* **38** B3
Vezdemarbán *E* **32** B2
Viana *E* **26** C2
Viana de Cega *E* **32** B3
Viana do Alentejo *P* **49** A4
Viana do Bolo *E* **23** D4
Viana do Castelo *P* **30** B2
Viaño Pequeno *E* **22** C2
Vianos *E* **42** D3
Viatodos *P* **30** B2
Viator *E* **59** A5
Vic *E* **37** A4
Vícar *E* **59** B4
Vicedo *E* **22** A3
Vich *E* **37** A4
Vidago *P* **31** B4
Vidais *P* **38** C2
Vidángoz *E* **27** C4
Videmonte *P* **31** D4
Vidigueira *P* **49** B4
Vidrieres *E* **37** A5
Vieira de Leiria *P* **38** B2
Vieira do Minho *P* **30** B3
Vielha *E* **28** C2
Vigo *E* **22** D2
Vila *E* **30** A3
Vila Boa *P* **31** D5
Vila Boa do Bispo *P* **30** C3
Vila Caiz *P* **30** B3
Vila Chã de Sá *P* **30** D3
Vila Cova da Lixa *P* **30** B3
Vilada *E* **28** D3
Viladamat *E* **29** D5
Vila da Ponte *P* **30** B3
Viladecans *E* **37** B4
Vila de Cruces *E* **22** C3
Vila de Frades *P* **49** B4
Vila de Rei *P* **38** B3
Vila do Bispo *P* **48** D2
Vila do Conde *P* **30** B2
Viladrau *E* **37** A4
Vilafant *E* **29** D5
Vila Fernando *P* **39** D5
Vila Flor *P* **31** B4
Vila Franca das Naves *P*
31 D4
Vilafranca del Penedès *E*
36 B3
Vila Franca de Xira *P* **38** D2
Vilagarcía de Arousa *E* **22** C2
Vilajuiga *E* **29** D5
Vilalba *E* **22** B3

Vilallonga *E* **29** D4
Vilamartín de Valdeorras *E*
23 D5
Vilamarxant *E* **43** B6
Vilamoura *P* **49** D4
Vila Nogueira de Azeitão *P*
48 A2
Vila Nova da Baronia *P*
49 A4
Vilanova d'Alcolea *E* **44** A3
Vilanova de Arousa *E* **22** C2
Vila Nova de Cacela *P* **49** D5
Vila Nova de Famalicão *P*
30 B2
Vila Nova de Foz Coa *P*
31 C4
Vila Nova de Gaia *P* **30** C2
Vilanova de la Barca *E* **36** B1
Vilanova de L'Aguda *E* **36** A2
Vilanova de Lourenzá *E*
23 B4
Vilanova de Meià *E* **28** D2
Vila Nova de Ourém *P*
38 B3
Vila Nova de Paiva *P* **30** C3
Vila Nova de Poiares *P* **38** A3
Vilanova de Prades *E* **36** B2
Vila Nova de São Bento *P*
49 B5
Vilanova de Sau *E* **37** A4
Vilanova i la Geltrú *E* **36** C3
Vila Pouca da Beira *P* **30** D3
Vila Pouca de Aguiar *P*
31 B4
Vila Praia de Âncora *P* **30** A1
Vilar *P* **30** A2
Vilar *P* **38** C2
Vilarandelo *P* **31** B4
Vilarchao *E* **22** D3
Vilar da Veiga *P* **30** B3
Vilar de Andorinho *P* **30** C2
Vilar de Barrio *E* **23** D4
Vilar de Santos *E* **22** D3
Vilardevós *E* **31** A4
Vila Real *P* **30** B3
Vila-real de los Infantes *E*
44 B3
Vila Real de Santo António *P*
49 D5
Vilarelho da Raia *P* **31** A4
Vilar Formoso *P* **31** D5
Vilarinho da Castanheira *P*
31 C4
Vilarinho do Bairro *P* **30** D2
Vilariño de Conso *E* **23** D4
Vila-rodona *E* **36** B2
Vila Ruiva *P* **49** B4
Vila Seca *P* **30** B2
Vilaseca de Solcina *E* **36** C2
Vilassar de Mar *E* **37** B4
Vila Velha de Ródão *P* **39** B4
Vila Verde *P* **30** B2
Vila Verde *P* **31** B4
Vila Verde *P* **38** A2
Vila Verde da Raia *P* **31** A4

Vila Verde de Ficalho *P* **49** B5
Vila Viçosa *P* **39** D5
Vilches *E* **52** B3
Villablanca *E* **49** D5
Villablino *E* **23** C6
Villabona *E* **26** B2
Villabrágima *E* **32** A2
Villabuena del Puente *E* **32** B2
Villacañas *E* **42** B1
Villacarlos *E* **47** B6
Villacarriedo *E* **25** B5
Villacarrillo *E* **52** B3
Villacastín *E* **33** D4
Villaciervos *E* **34** A1
Villaconejos *E* **41** A6
Villaconejos de Trabaque *E* **34** D2
Villada *E* **24** D3
Villa del Prado *E* **41** A5
Villa del Río *E* **51** B5
Villadepera *E* **31** B6
Villa de Ves *E* **43** C5
Villadiego *E* **25** C4
Villaeles de Valdavia *E* **24** C3
Villaescusa de Haro *E* **42** B3
Villaescusa la Sombría *E* **25** D5
Villafáfila *E* **32** A2
Villafamés *E* **44** A3
Villafeliche *E* **34** C3
Villaflores *E* **32** C2
Villafranca de Bonany *E* **47** B4
Villafranca de Córdoba *E* **51** B5
Villafranca de Ebro *E* **35** B5
Villafranca del Bierzo *E* **23** C5
Villafranca del Campo *E* **34** D3
Villafranca del Cid *E* **35** D5
Villafranca de los Barros *E* **50** A2
Villafranca de los Caballeros *E* **42** C1
Villafranca-Montes de Oca *E* **25** D5
Villafranco del Guadalquivir *E* **50** D2
Villafrechos *E* **32** A2
Villafruela *E* **33** A4
Villafuerte *E* **33** A4
Villagarcía de Campos *E* **32** A2
Villagarcía de la Torre *E* **50** A2
Villagarcía del Llano *E* **43** C4
Villagonzalo *E* **40** D1
Villaharta *E* **51** B4
Villahermosa *E* **42** D2
Villahermosa del Campo *E* **35** C4
Villahermosa del Río *E* **44** A2

Villaherreros *E* **24** D3
Villahizán *E* **25** D5
Villahoz *E* **25** D4
Villajoyosa - La Vila Joíosa *E* **55** A4
Villalar de los Comuneros *E* **32** B2
Villalba de Duero *E* **33** B5
Villalba de Guardo *E* **24** C3
Villalba del Alcor *E* **49** C6
Villalba de la Sierra *E* **43** A4
Villalba de los Alcores *E* **32** A3
Villalba de los Barros *E* **39** D6
Villalba del Rey *E* **34** D1
Villalba dels Arcs *E* **35** C6
Villalba de Rioja *E* **25** C6
Villalcampo *E* **31** B6
Villalcázar de Sirga *E* **24** D3
Villalengua *E* **34** B3
Villalgordo del Júcar *E* **43** C4
Villalobos *E* **32** A2
Villalón de Campos *E* **24** D3
Villalonga *E* **44** D3
Villalpando *E* **32** A2
Villalpardo *E* **43** C4
Villaluenga de la Sagra *E* **41** A6
Villalumbroso *E* **24** D3
Villamalea *E* **43** C4
Villamañán *E* **24** D2
Villamandos *E* **24** D2
Villamanrique *E* **53** A4
Villamanrique de la Condesa *E* **50** D2
Villamanta *E* **41** A5
Villamartín *E* **57** B4
Villamartín de Campos *E* **32** A3
Villamayor *E* **32** C1
Villamayor de Calatrava *E* **41** D5
Villamayor de Campos *E* **32** A2
Villamayor de Santiago *E* **42** B2
Villamayor de Treviño *E* **25** D4
Villamediana *E* **25** D4
Villamediana de Iregua *E* **26** D2
Villamejil *E* **23** C6
Villamesías *E* **40** C2
Villamiel *E* **39** A6
Villamor de los Escuderos *E* **32** C2
Villamuelas *E* **41** B6
Villamuriel de Cerrato *E* **32** A3
Villanúa *E* **27** C5
Villanubla *E* **32** B3
Villanueva de Alcardete *E* **42** B2
Villanueva de Alcorón *E* **34** D2

Villanueva de Algaidas *E* **51** D5
Villanueva de Argaño *E* **25** D4
Villanueva de Bogas *E* **41** B6
Villanueva de Cameros *E* **26** D1
Villanueva de Castellón *E* **43** C6
Villanueva de Córdoba *E* **51** A5
Villanueva de Gállego *E* **35** A4
Villanueva de Gómez *E* **32** C3
Villanueva de la Cañada *E* **33** D4
Villanueva de la Concepción *E* **51** D5
Villanueva de la Fuente *E* **42** D3
Villanueva de la Jara *E* **43** C4
Villanueva de la Reina *E* **51** B6
Villanueva de las Cruces *E* **49** C6
Villanueva de la Serena *E* **40** D2
Villanueva de la Sierra *E* **39** A6
Villanueva de las Torres *E* **52** C3
Villanueva de la Vera *E* **40** A3
Villanueva del Campo *E* **32** A2
Villanueva del Duque *E* **51** A4
Villanueva del Fresno *E* **49** A5
Villanueva de los Castillejos *E* **49** C5
Villanueva de los Infantes *E* **42** D2
Villanueva del Rey *E* **51** B4
Villanueva del Río Segura *E* **54** B2
Villanueva del Río y Minas *E* **50** C3
Villanueva del Rosario *E* **51** D5
Villanueva del Trabuco *E* **51** D5
Villanueva de Mesía *E* **51** D6
Villanueva de San Carlos *E* **41** D6
Villanueva de San Juan *E* **51** D4
Villanueva de Tapia *E* **51** D5
Villanueva de Valdegovia *E* **25** C6
Villanuño de Valdavia *E* **24** C3

Villapalacios *E* **53** A4
Villaquejida *E* **24** D2
Villaquilambre *E* **24** C2
Villaralbo *E* **32** B1
Villaralto *E* **51** A4
Villarcayo *E* **25** C5
Villar de Cañas *E* **42** B3
Villar de Chinchilla *E* **43** D5
Villar de Ciervo *E* **31** D5
Villardeciervos *E* **31** A6
Villardefrades *E* **32** B2
Villar del Arzobispo *E* **43** B6
Villar de la Yegua *E* **31** D5
Villar del Buey *E* **31** B6
Villar del Cobo *E* **34** D3
Villar del Humo *E* **43** B4
Villar de los Barrios *E* **23** D5
Villar de los Navarros *E* **35** C4
Villar del Pedroso *E* **40** B3
Villar del Rey *E* **39** C6
Villar del Salz *E* **34** D3
Villar de Olalla *E* **42** B3
Villar de Peralonso *E* **31** C6
Villar de Rena *E* **40** C2
Villar de Torre *E* **25** D6
Villardompardo *E* **51** B6
Villarejo de Fuentes *E* **42** B3
Villarejo de Montalbán *E* **41** B4
Villarejo de Orbigo *E* **23** D6
Villarejo de Salvanés *E* **42** A2
Villarente *E* **24** C2
Villares de la Reina *E* **32** C1
Villargordo *E* **51** B6
Villargordo del Cabriel *E* **43** C5
Villarino de los Aires *E* **31** B6
Villarluengo *E* **35** D5
Villarquemado *E* **35** D4
Villarramiel *E* **24** D3
Villarrasa *E* **49** C6
Villarreal de Huerva *E* **35** C4
Villarrín de Campos *E* **32** A2
Villarrobledo *E* **42** C3
Villarrodrigo *E* **53** A4
Villarroya de la Sierra *E* **34** B3
Villarroya de los Pinares *E* **35** D5
Villarrubia de los Ojos *E* **41** C6
Villarrubia de Santiago *E* **41** A6
Villarrubio *E* **42** B2
Villars del Saz *E* **42** B3
Villarta *E* **43** C4
Villarta de los Montes *E* **41** C4
Villarta de San Juan *E* **41** C6
Villasana de Mena *E* **25** B5
Villasandino *E* **25** D4
Villasante de Montija *E* **25** B5

Villasarracino *E* **24** D3
Villasayas *E* **34** B1
Villasbuenas *E* **31** C5
Villasdardo *E* **31** C6
Villaseca de Laciana *E* **23** C6
Villaseca de la Sagra *E* **41** B6
Villaseco de los Gamitos *E* **31** C6
Villaseco de los Reyes *E* **31** C6
Villaseco del Pan *E* **31** B6
Villasequilla de Yepes *E* **41** B6
Villasrubias *E* **31** D5
Villastar *E* **43** A5
Villasur de Herreros *E* **25** D5
Villatobas *E* **42** B1
Villatoro *E* **32** D2
Villatoya *E* **43** C5
Villatuerta *E* **26** C2
Villaturiel *E* **24** C2
Villaumbrales *E* **24** D3
Villava *E* **26** C3
Villavelayo *E* **25** D6
Villaverde de Guadalimar *E* **53** A4
Villaverde del Río *E* **50** C2
Villaverde y Pasaconsol *E* **42** B3
Villaviciosa *E* **24** A2
Villaviciosa de Córdoba *E* **51** B4
Villaviciosa de Odón *E* **33** D5
Villavieja *E* **44** B3
Villavieja de Yeltes *E* **31** C6
Villaviudas *E* **33** A4
Villayón *E* **23** B5
Villazanzo de Valderaduey *E* **24** C3
Villegas *E* **25** D4
Villel *E* **43** A5
Villena *E* **43** D6
Villerías *E* **32** A3
Villoldo *E* **24** D3
Villora *E* **43** B4
Villoria *E* **32** C2
Villoruela *E* **32** C2
Viloví d'Onyar *E* **37** A5

Vilvestre *E* **31** C5
Vimbodi *E* **36** B2
Vimeiro *P* **38** C1
Vimianzo *E* **22** B1
Vimieiro *P* **39** D4
Vimioso *P* **31** B5
Vinaixa *E* **36** B2
Vinaròs *E* **36** D1
Vinaroz *E* **36** D1
Vinebre *E* **36** C1
Vinhais *P* **31** A5
Vinhas *P* **31** B5
Viniegra de Arriba *E* **25** D6
Viñuelas *E* **33** C5
Vinuesa *E* **33** A6
Viseu *P* **30** D3
Visiedo *E* **35** D4
Viso del Marqués *E* **52** A3
Vistabella del Maestrazgo *E* **44** A2
Vitigudino *E* **31** C6
Vitoria-Gasteiz *E* **27** C1
Viveiro *E* **23** A4
Vivel del Río Martín *E* **35** C4
Viver *E* **43** B6
Vivero *E* **23** A4
Viveros *E* **42** D3
Vouzela *P* **30** D3
Vozmediano *E* **34** A3

W

Wamba *E* **32** B3

X

Xanceda *E* **22** B3
Xátiva *E* **43** D6
Xeraco *E* **44** D3
Xeresa *E* **44** D3
Xermade *E* **22** B3
Xerta *E* **36** C1
Xinzo de Limia *E* **30** A3
Xirivella *E* **44** C2
Xove *E* **23** A4
Xunqueira de Ambía *E* **22** D3

Y

Yanguas *E* **26** D2
Yatova *E* **43** C6
Yebra *E* **33** D6
Yebra de Basa *E* **27** C5
Yecla *E* **43** D5
Yecla de Yeltes *E* **31** C6
Yémeda *E* **43** B4
Yepes *E* **41** B6
Yesa *E* **27** C4
Yeste *E* **53** A5
Yuncler *E* **41** A6
Yuncos *E* **41** A6
Yunquera *E* **57** B5
Yunquera de Henares *E* **33** D6

Z

Zafarraya *E* **51** D6
Zafra *E* **50** A1
Zafra de Záncara *E* **42** B3
Zafrilla *E* **43** A4
Zagra *E* **51** D5
Zahara *E* **57** B4
Zahara de los Atunes *E* **56** C3
Zahinos *E* **49** A6
Zaidín *E* **35** B6
Zalamea de la Serena *E* **40** D2
Zalamea la Real *E* **49** C6
Zaldibar *E* **26** B1
Zambrana *E* **25** C6
Zambujal de Cima *P* **48** A2
Zambujeira do Mar *P* **48** C2
Zamora *E* **32** B1
Zaorejas *E* **34** D2
Zaragoza *E* **35** B4
Zaratamo *E* **25** B6
Zaratán *E* **32** B3
Zarautz *E* **26** B2
Zarauz *E* **26** B2
Zarcilla de Ramos *E* **53** B6
Zarra *E* **43** C5
Zarza Capilla *E* **40** D3

Zarza de Alange *E* **40** D1
Zarza de Granadilla *E* **40** A2
Zarza de Tajo *E* **42** B2
Zarzadilla de Totana *E* **53** B6
Zarza la Mayor *E* **39** B6
Zarzuela del Monte *E* **33** C4
Zarzuela del Pinar *E* **33** B4
Zas *E* **22** B1
Zebreira *P* **39** B5
Zegama *E* **26** B2
Zestoa *E* **26** B2
Zibreira *P* **38** C3
Zizurkil *E* **26** B2
Zorita *E* **40** C2
Zorita del Maestrazgo *E* **35** D5
Zornotza *E* **25** B6
Zuazo de Cuartango *E* **25** C6
Zubia *E* **52** D2
Zubiaur *E* **25** B6
Zubieta *E* **26** B2
Zubieta *E* **26** B3
Zubiri *E* **26** C3
Zucaina *E* **44** A2
Zudaire *E* **26** C2
Zuera *E* **35** A4
Zufre *E* **50** B2
Zuheros *E* **51** C5
Zújar *E* **53** C4
Zumaia *E* **26** B2
Zumarraga *E* **26** B2
Zunzarren *E* **26** C3
Zúrgena *E* **53** D5